THE DAY
I DIED
& FOUND
ANXIETY

Travis Garza

ACKNOWLEDGEMENTS

I want to thank my Lord Jesus Christ for giving me the words to create this book in hopes of helping others who suffer from anxiety.

This book is dedicated to my mom Anne Mason who has always wanted me to write a book.

To my wife Adrea Garza, who stuck by my side day and night during the long eight months of suffering, when my anxiety was at its highest.

To my sister Bea Jaye, who is a nurse practitioner, for answering never-ending questions about what was going on with me, during my most fearful moments of those eight months.

To my first daughter, Sydney, who came to the heart hospital and gave me courage at a time I had none. Thank you for being strong for me.

To my twin daughters Haven and Koti, who along with Sydney, gave me a stronger motivation to get better to be there for them.

To Hannah my niece, Chris my brother-in-law, and Max my good friend and husband to my mom, I'm grateful to have each of you as part of my family and support system.

To my Doctor and good friend, Dr. Bruce Daniels. Thanks for always taking time to talk to me regardless of how many times to make me feel better.

TABLE OF CONTENTS

●   ●   ●   ●   ●

INTRODUCTION

Monday, January 8, 2018, I woke up like any other day at 5:00 a.m. to get ready for my morning workout while everyone else in the house was asleep. When I sat up, something was drastically different about the way I felt. I stood up and went to the bathroom to wash my face as I always do and then the realization that something wasn't right set in.

I was experiencing something I had never felt in my life and had no explanation for. Immediately, fear set in and my heart started racing. I started replaying what I had eaten the day before, asking myself if this was food poisoning? Had I caught some kind of virus? Or was I just exhausted and needed some rest?

My thoughts were all over the place trying to find the answer to justify my fear of what was going on. I proceeded to my workout, thinking this will all go away once I get a workout in and clear my head. As I started my workout, I found myself more focused on things going back to normal than the workout itself. As the workout continued and nothing was changing, little did I know at that moment, I would begin an eight-month (silent) journey of trying to make sense of how I was feeling.

The only thing I could compare to the way I felt was being in a dream and while I was in my body, I wasn't really *in* my body. I was watching what my body was doing from the outside looking in. I was speaking to people, but didn't really feel like it was me talking to them. I was a bystander observing the conversation, yet it was me talking. My strong-willed mind that had served me for years, tried to convince me "you're ok" to calm the fear, but the logical part of my mind was telling me different.

It was telling me this is not ok and you don't understand what's happening. I went home that morning after my workout and decided it best to keep this to myself, (even from my wife). I told myself, get it together, you're responsible for taking care of your wife, three daughters, the bills and running three companies.

You cannot let anyone know you feel afraid, but don't know what of and that your thoughts are all over the place. I lived my life like this for one month, before opening up to my wife and then my mom about what had been going on.

Immediately, they made me go to my doctor to have tests ran. Each one of them coming back as 100% normal. If I only knew what was wrong with me, I could at least deal with it versus the unknown. With my wife and mom by my side for support, we spent the next seven months battling my condition in private (per my request), trying everything we could to make sense of what was going on. I would have what I started calling "better days" and then what I can only label as horrible days, where I felt like I was going out of my mind. My heart would race, blood pressure skyrocket and my thoughts ran out of control with panic.

One evening while eating, my chest started tightening up and I felt like I couldn't breathe. I convinced myself it was nothing and it would go away. My wife and mom decided differently. My mom drove 30 minutes late in the evening to my house, walked into the kitchen and said, "You can either let us drive you to the heart hospital or I will call 911 and have an ambulance take you there." I broke down crying. I had finally reached my breaking point. Nobody and no situation in my 52 years of living, had ever broken me before, but this "thing" I was experiencing had. My wife drove me to the heart hospital and we checked in. They asked me a series of questions and put me in a bed. They were calm and I could tell by their demeanor they were not alarmed by my situation. It was as if they had seen this before.

As they were starting an IV and hooking me up to several machines, I started feeling faint and told my wife I was going to pass out. My hearing went first and then a bright white light appeared. It filled the room and a feeling of warmth overcame me. I remember feeling great and completely at ease. This feeling was something I hadn't felt in what seemed like forever. As I embraced this feeling of warmth and comfort, I noticed the white light leaving and I started seeing the ceiling of a room that I wasn't familiar with.

Then I saw people yelling at me and my wife being pulled into the hallway. I was trying so hard to figure out what was going on, but couldn't. As the people were yelling at me, I slowly started hearing them and feeling this excruciating pain in my chest. They were yelling, "Travis can you hear us?" over and over again. I finally was able to answer them... "Yes, I can." A series of questions were being asked to see if I could answer. I then saw my wife crying her eyes out and what appeared to be 10 medical personnel in the room with me. I asked what happened? The response was your heart stopped beating and you were gone for six seconds. They didn't rule it as a heart attack, but that my heart just spontaneously stopped. In other words, I died for six seconds.

For two days, they kept me in bed not allowing me to get up. I was hooked up to the latest and greatest that technology has to offer in order to find the answers. I had every blood, urine and organ test known to man performed on me. They ran a catheter through my wrist to check out my heart and arteries. I told myself, I was finally going to find out what was wrong with me. They would prescribe me some medication and I would be back to my normal life. The final day at the heart hospital as I awaited for some answers an older lady, who I assumed was a nurse, came in. During my stay, I had seen too many different people and doctors to count, but had never seen her. Little did I know at the time that what she said next would come to define my life forever. She placed her hand on my head and said, "Son...nothing is wrong with you...you have anxiety."

I laughed at this as I told her, "I speak in front of hundreds of people and love it. I don't get worked up over things or worry." She said there is much more to anxiety than that. She left the room and a counselor came in to discuss some things that had to change in my life, if I wanted things to get better. I took his list and that's where I started my journey to discover if I fit the definition of anxiety and what to do about it.

I walked into a world that I didn't even know existed. I was the poster child for anxiety and learned all the forms it comes in and what it stems from. I have spent over a year learning everything I can about anxiety and how to overcome it. How to live with it. How to be aware of what triggers it or fuels it.

This book is to help you immediately get back to a better life and not spend months as I did in silence, learning how to overcome it. First, I am going to let you know you're ok and you're not alone in the midst of the unknown. Anxiety is a human, shared emotion we all experience on one level or another. I spent months being silent and keeping it bottled up inside. The first step to recovery and relief is to talk about what you're experiencing with someone you trust.

In the following chapters, I want to guide you using several tools I personally used and still do today, that have helped me on my road to recovery from anxiety.

I want to show you how to get your values in order and why this lowers your anxiety. How creating structure in your life creates space in the mind that reduces anxiety. Why the food you eat dictates the intensity of your anxiety. Why exercising in the morning lowers anxiety. Why going to bed and getting up at a certain time lowers anxiety. I will show you how meditating is my number one tool in keeping anxiety away. I will show you how journaling for anxiety will break that thought in your mind, that you're not getting better.

How being grateful and learning that anxiety cannot exist in a grateful mindset. Why you need to surround yourself with people you feel at peace with.

How adding value to someone's life daily doesn't allow anxiety to be present. Why you can't live your life waiting for the anxiety to go away. Why we must live each day in the present and not worry about tomorrow. Tomorrow will take care of itself. Finally, I want you to understand something I failed at several times, before realizing the truth. You can't control anxiety with a quick fix band-aid approach. It will go away and your first reaction is it's gone and I can go back to my old way of life. It will return. You must accept that you must change some things in your life forever and that may mean giving up some things in your old life that were the underlying cause of your anxiety.

I have found over time, the changes I was resistant to simply because I felt my old life had been taken from me, resulted in a much more peaceful life. One that I could have never imagined. A peaceful life yet more productive than ever. Let me take you one step at a time to a better quality of life both mentally and physically.

I want you to know I'm here for you every step of the way. You're ok...you just have anxiety

CHAPTER 1

You're Not Alone

For over eight months, I experienced something that I don't want anyone to have to go through. I landed in a dark place I didn't think I was going to ever get out of. A place we are not hard-wired to deal with regardless of how tough we may think we are. A place where we are left to rationalize our thoughts and figure things out good or bad. A place where eventually your thoughts could lead you down a bad path. That place is called... being alone.

I was brought up to handle things myself and not depend on anyone for anything. If I had a problem, I was taught to deal with it or fix it and not complain about it to anyone. If I had a headache, I was taught to take an aspirin and continue on. All my life, I depended on myself to get things done. I never paid much attention to what everyone else was doing.

You can say I marched to the beat of my own drum. In my opinion, that is why I was so successful in my business. Whatever problems came to me in life, I never stopped to ask myself if this had happened to anyone else, if they have an explanation for it and a way to solve it or make it better? Why would I? My method had served me well for 51 years. I was completely self-absorbed. Not in the ego format as some may use that word, but in a way of truly not looking around to see what everyone else may be going through or experiencing.

Since I was taught to deal with my own problems and not complain, I assumed everyone else was supposed to do the same. My approach centered on internalizing all of life's problems and figuring out a solution on your own because if you did complain or tell someone else, it was a sign of weakness.

On January 8, 2018, when I woke up that morning and something drastically was wrong, I began my eight-month journey of internalizing how I felt and would go to work, figuring it out alone. From day one, I had already made up my mind that this was an isolated incident happening only to me that nobody else had ever experienced. The only person that could help me was myself.

I said to myself that I had been in many bad situations in life and my desire and drive to overcome it always won. This was going to be no different, but each day the battle was a little different. I would wake up and try and get a grip on how I was feeling, while trying to ignore my thoughts of trying to rationalize what was wrong with me as they ran wild with panic and fear.

My daily routine always began with cooking breakfast for my two-year-old twins, a task I love to do. Sadly, I found myself struggling just to get through the act of doing it. It was so overwhelming to the point where I would occasionally have to make an excuse to go into the other room to gather my thoughts. I would take a deep breath and splash water on my face, while looking in the mirror telling myself, "Travis pull it together. Your kids depend on you."

I would return to making breakfast and silently in my mind wanting this to be over so I could retreat to the bathroom and be alone again. Being alone was easy at first, I didn't have to summon up the strength to put on an act while talking to my wife or kids. So, getting ready for work was a "break" if you want to call it that. Driving to work was an entirely new battle for me.

I found myself tensing up, gripping the steering wheel and my fear off the chart. What was I afraid of? Why did I fear something I could not identify? I searched my mind relentlessly looking for answers. In my entire career in the fitness industry, people have always made the comment, "I have never seen a person love getting up and going to his job as Travis does even after 35 plus years of doing it." That had changed overnight.

I now struggled just to get in the front door and the thought of having a meeting with my staff terrified me to the point of having severe stomach aches and throwing up. Who was this person that loved his job and his staff, but now was bent over in the bathroom scared to the point of passing out with just the thought of interacting with them? I once again resorted to splashing water on my face looking in the mirror telling myself, "Travis pull it together. Your business and employees depend on you as a leader."

I put on a front while at work like everything was ok trying to lead my company. I would retreat to the bathroom when I couldn't take it anymore just like I did at home and then return when I willed the strength to do so. As I spoke to my staff, I wondered if they could see through the front and see the fear in my eyes and how I really felt. I love being able to perform many tasks at once and always creating new programs for my business, Garza's Fat Loss Camp.

I found this ability had disappeared overnight. I now wanted to get through the day and do only what was needed. In my mind, I was only worried about how long I can continue this act before completely falling apart in front of my staff. When the day ended, you would think the thought of going home to see my wife and twins Koti and Haven, would put a smile on my face. What I experienced was just the opposite.

As I entered the gates of my development, an alarm of fear went off to unbelievable heights. Again, the rational side of me asked, "Travis what are you so afraid of?" As I performed the duty of being a Dad and trying to emotionally engage with my daughters, I found myself retreating often to the bathroom for the ritual of splashing water on my face and self-talk. I would make excuses to take out the trash, do laundry, empty the dishwasher, anything, but have to interact with my family. It simply was too overwhelming.

After the kids went to bed, I would escape to the bathroom for a shower to be alone. I found that in the evening time, the fear wasn't as elevated as it was in the morning and during the day. As the days went by and I experienced less fear in the evenings on a regular basis, I began to have a fear of going to bed, knowing when I woke up from what little sleep I was getting, it would start all over again. It was like I was experiencing the movie Groundhog Day every day for eight months. In Groundhog Day, actor Bill Murray gets stuck in a world that he repeats each day exactly as the day before. Until one moment he came to the realization, that he needed to think less about himself and more about others. This was the day that changed it all for him.

The weekends for the last 12 years had been something I looked forward to with great excitement and joy, watching my 15-year-old daughter, Sydney, play soccer. I loved taking her and her soccer mates to games, traveling to other states and staying at hotels. This had also changed overnight.

The thought of traveling, talking to her and cheering her on at games elevated my fear once again. The voice of logic was still fighting so hard to understand and was once again asking, "Travis what is wrong with you? This is Sydney who you have been with since the beginning of her soccer journey and love every moment of it. What are you afraid of?" Faking being a dad to my two-year-old twins Koti and Haven was easier to wrap my head around, as they were not of age to understand yet. Sydney and I have an amazing relationship and we know each other inside and out. This was not going to be so easy. My biggest fear was Sydney ever knowing what I was going through. I am a Dad, the protector, provider and one to help her with her problems. Not the other way around. I wasn't going to let her see this weakness (as I labeled it then), I had.

The person I couldn't avoid easily or have a brief conversation with and leave, was my wife Adrea. This is a woman that had known me for many years, my traits, my habits and routines. I'm known (especially by her), as a routine person, so any break in the routine is a red flag especially around her. I had always worked out at 5:00

a.m. before the girls get up and since the day this all began, I had not stepped foot back in the gym.

Working out had become a fear in my mind I felt would intensify my unknown situation. I had no reason behind it, but then again I had no reason behind anything I was feeling or doing during this time. I started fearing certain foods were making my unknown feeling worse, so I cut out having our weekly Saturday cheat meals, which regularly included What-a-Burger and Krispy Kreme doughnuts. I had concluded in my mind that eating perfect would help me, although I had no reason behind this thinking at the time. And so began an eight-month journey of living off pretty much nothing but eggs, chicken, rice, and water.

I had become very quiet at home and only talked if I had to. My wife was not pressing me for answers, but I was well aware by her demeanor that the Travis she had known for years wasn't present. For one month from the day, everything changed. I had kept the unknown, indescribable feeling and fear to myself. As time passed and the fear of the unknown grew in strength, I finally broke down crying one evening to my wife.

I told her I didn't know what was wrong with me and I was scared beyond belief. That I went to bed two months ago on a Sunday and woke the next day living in a completely different world. I made her swear this was our secret and nobody was to know, including my mom. We tried to backtrack my steps to anything different that I had done. Nothing. My routine was so strict that it was easy to see nothing was out of the ordinary except what I was experiencing. She worked with me day and night helping me to summons up enough courage to get through each day. Months went by. I went to different doctors looking for an answer. Each one with different tests and opinions, all of them ultimately saying there is nothing wrong with you.

I had become so scared and obsessed with finding out what was wrong with me that I lost touch with reality in some ways. I would go to the doctor's with charts and pages of notes to be sure I didn't leave anything out in regards to what was going on each hour of the day, what I suspected made me feel better and the crazy theories of what had happened to me. To them, I could tell I sounded like a mad man by the look on their faces and the disregard to my well-prepared presentation. Test after test was completed over the next several months all concluding that I was perfectly fine.

At first, you fear what a doctor may find wrong with you and then over a period of time, you start hoping the next doctor will have a diagnosis. At least I would know what I was dealing with, which is way better than the daily fear of the unknown. You see, I kept looking for what was wrong with me based on test results. I never considered that what I was going through wasn't an isolated feeling or unique to only myself.

I never considered that the people around me could be going through something similar that I could have identified and connected with. When we are going through something, it's very easy to only look inward and not outward. It's very easy for us to be fixated on ourselves. Being alone with our thoughts when we don't understand or can't get answers from the doctors as to what's going on starts a vicious unhealthy cycle downward.

Being alone with something you don't understand in your mind can grow to terrify you. The worst part is, you can't find the words to explain to someone what you're feeling emotionally and physically without sounding crazy. The unknown can bring thoughts, emotions, and mainly fear to the surface of your thoughts. Trying to explain the unknown is like trying to explain to your dog why biting that electrical cord isn't good. At this point, I really started isolating myself into my mind trying to figure out what was wrong with me. My fear led the way 90% of the time with every possible scenario of what was happening.

My thoughts would race from, it will get better over time to maybe your hormones are out of balance. To having some kind of disease, you may have to live the rest of your life with or you have gone insane. The next day it would start all over again. It's very important that you understand something right now before we move forward. What I'm about to tell you did not fix my underlying problem in itself, however, it did give me some immediate comfort.

Comfort I had prayed for over eight months to receive, even if it was only a ray of light. I wish today I would have had someone give me this information from the beginning, so I could at least feel some sort of peace and focus on a solution. But then again, I wasn't looking, I was to busy dealing with it on my own. Once equipped with this information and starting to look outside of myself to others experiencing the same thing, my perspective changed.

My hope is that this will change your perspective and give you some comfort moving forward. What I learned is that I'm not alone. The truth is, what I was experiencing is a human shared emotion named anxiety. The problem exists for people from all walks of life including business owners, executives, and entrepreneurs. Anxiety can even take down your favorite celebrity.

In a 2011 *Rolling Stone* article, superstar and vocalist, Adele admitted to having frequent anxiety attacks before and during her shows. Even Bono, the lead singer of U2- despite 25 years of selling out stadiums, struggles with anxiety. Anxiety can affect everyone. Anxiety can bring anyone to their knees. It doesn't matter how tough you are. Anxiety doesn't care what you have done or how much you've got to do today. Anxiety is an emotion like happiness, sadness and fear. Anxiety, which is fear driven, is an emotion we need to alarm us to run, getaway or be on guard.

Its job is to protect us from harm, but when it is active continually is when it becomes a problem. The problem is the uncertainty, unpredictability and a sense of the unknown around anxiety. The person, such as myself, typically suffers and struggles in silence, not knowing what exactly is happening or what to do about it. All they know for sure is that they feel like they are having the worst day of their life and don't know when that feeling is going to end. When you realize you're not alone and you're sharing an emotion that everyone has to one degree or the other, it brings things into focus.

Anxiety is an increasingly (common) mental health issue that affects over forty million Americans and growing according to a June 2017, *New York Times* article. There are likely millions more who also suffer from anxiety and haven't yet (identified) it, or sought help for it, simply because they can't understand what it is, or they are scared of being shamed for it. Sound familiar? Anxiety is complex and affects people in different ways.

It comes in the form of panic attacks that may be temporary, situational anxiety, to everyday overall anxiety. Knowing I wasn't alone, allowed me to start focusing on the underlying problem. What was causing me to have anxiety? What steps could I take to get it under control? This gave me a renewed sense of living with a purpose. To read as much material as I could get my hands on, listen to those that were experiencing it, listen to every audio tape dealing with anxiety and pray to God for understanding it all.

To one day be in a stable enough position to help someone else. To give them the tools that worked for me to help them regain their life. Before moving forward, if you are experiencing what I was, I want to refer you to your doctor. Get all the tests done and once you have been cleared as "in good health" that's when the strategies in this book and my advice, based on my own personal experience, can help. I want to be totally transparent with you so you know you're not alone.

As I write this book, I am sharing with you every tool I have along with all the knowledge I still use on myself today to manage my anxiety. We are going to work through this together and you're going to be ok. As soon as you truly believe you are not alone and can overcome this- you'll put yourself on the road to finding a better quality of life, a life I am committed to walking with you

CHAPTER 2

Understanding What Anxiety Is

I'm of the belief if you understand what something is and how it works, then you can better relate to it. For example, I explain to my clients at Garza's Fat Loss Camps how the body truly burns fat. Blood sugar must be stabilized through my eating plan and then the fat is released into the bloodstream. Once the fat is in the bloodstream, my 40-minute workout only using 5lb dumbbells will burn the fat.

This makes the process of losing weight so much easier because my clients are now educated on how you truly lose weight and burn body fat. The process of learning about anything that affects you and your life helps you to fully connect with the process. So if you begin to understand anxiety and not that it just makes your life miserable, you start to build a relationship with it instead of always fighting it. The more we fight anxiety, the more the mind brings it to your attention and the more your focus is shifted solely on the anxiety itself.

Making friends with anxiety may sound completely irrational since we are wired to fight or reject anything that is not pleasing to our well-being, but if you change that perspective and actually look at it with curiosity, wanting to understand it, the effects of it will dial back to a manageable level. Imagine having a fight with your best friend. It goes on for weeks and it stays on your mind 99% of the time.

All you can think about is the fight you're having with your friend, how much you hate it and the fact that it's making your life miserable. If you decided to change your perspective on what you don't like about your friend to truly trying to understand her for what she is, then how would you feel? I would say better. It doesn't mean you are completely ok with her and her actions, but you're in a better place now than before when you were 100% resistant.

I want you to start looking at anxiety like this. You don't have to like it and how its making you feel, I get it. However, if we start looking at it from an approach of curiosity and understanding, we find the anxiety in itself starts to fall apart to a lesser degree. Trying to fight anxiety does nothing, but fuel it. So you may be wondering "Travis are you asking me to make friends with anxiety?" My answer is yes to some extent. Doesn't the thought of the words "making friends" kind of give you a good feeling? Say the words out loud, "Making friends." The emotion after saying that typically is a feel-good one.

Anxiety is the same thing, an emotion. It's not some weird disease you have or unexplained virus the world has never seen. Anxiety has been around for as long as humans have been alive. Like any other emotion, it's neither good nor bad. It's just part of a normal range of emotions that affect everyone. And for some people, it can be dialed up just a little too high. Our society has labeled it something to be very afraid of and to keep quiet about if you have it. To the point that if you let people know about it, you run the risk of wearing a big red A on your sleeve letting the world know what you have.

I am by no means downplaying the effects of anxiety or making light of it. I want you to help me try and change the world's perspective on anxiety to a perspective and approach of curiosity and observation. Look at this viewpoint. Let's say there is a major storm consisting of rain, lightning, and strong winds and you're standing outside in the middle of it. You're getting wet, blown around and feeling all of the effects. Now let's say you're inside your house looking out of a window viewing the same storm.

You're looking at the storm with curiosity in regards to the rain, lightning, and wind. These are two totally different ways to experience the same storm. This is how I want you to approach your anxiety with curiosity, not being caught up in it. Most importantly, understanding that everyone in the world has this emotion to one degree or the other.

It's one of the most talked-about emotions today in a very negative and labeling manner. What you will not hear people talking about is, "Do you know that Travis has that happy emotion?" However after reading this book people will ask, "Did you know that Travis has that anxiety emotion?" That's because it's been labeled a disease or the very comforting words "mental health disorder."

Now the words "mental health disorder" make you feel like you're perfectly normal right? Of all the books, audios, articles and interviews with specialists on the topic of anxiety, the one thing they all had in common was everyone has anxiety just like every other emotion we share as humans.

I want you to let that sink in as I hope it gives you some immediate comfort as it did me. I now am so hyper focused on the topic, I see people everywhere coming out and talking about their battle with anxiety. I see pro Basketball players, NFL football players and many of my clients at Garza's Fat Loss Camps talking about it. Most recently, as I write this book, the pastor my church Life Church, Craig Groeschel, revealed in a sermon that he was battling anxiety.

He stated he had known several people over the years that were dealing with it, but had never experienced it before himself. My point here is not to express that knowing other people have anxiety makes me happy. It only serves to let me know I'm not alone in dealing with this. Since that is the case, if I can help people learn to exist in some sort of harmony with this emotion, it's been worth what I went through. During my quest to understand this emotion so I could relate to it and understand why my version of anxiety was on full blast 24 hours a day, I started with the basics of how our mind uses anxiety under normal circumstances.

Anxiety under normal circumstances comes about in the presence of danger or worry of the unknown. If you are being followed by a man with a knife, your adrenaline kicks in and your anxiety goes up better related to as fear. Your body is protecting you by giving you the energy, (adrenaline) and kicking in your emotion of fear (anxiety) to remove you from the life-threatening situation, aka run for your life. Your body has given you supernatural energy, (adrenaline) and the emotion of fear (anxiety) to make you respond in a very serious manner.

It's when this emotion turns on and doesn't shut off that it becomes a problem. A good friend of mine, Dr. Bruce Daniels when asked what has caused my anxiety to turn on and stay on, he responded with this. "Travis I see it all the time. It's from a life of "Unremitting stress." Now those two words, I could really identify with. It sums up my 51 years of living. He compared it to having a miniature form of PTSD. He followed that up with the words, "It's a very common thing. I see it all the time." So how does unremitting stress cause anxiety?

While at dinner one night in California on a business trip, the topic of anxiety came up amongst a group of my colleagues. I listened to this conversation as many of them had their opinion, mostly negative except one. This individual spoke of helping people dealing with PTSD and anxiety by diving into the subconscious. The subconscious? That's that part of the brain we don't use right?

As I showed interest and explained my situation, the conversation turned solely to him and I. He explained that our subconscious is like one big recording of our life. It records and stores every experience that takes place in our life, good and bad. From the ages of 3-8, what your subconscious records, (life experiences) basically results in the way you will view the world moving forward. He explained that a lot of things that cause us anxiety today are a direct result of something that happened in our childhood. The subconscious brings this to the surface in the form of anxiety.

Some events that you can recall as if it were yesterday from your early childhood most likely made an impact on your life forever. You may not think that event has anything to do with your anxiety consciously thinking, but if you become curious about why that memory is so clear in your mind after all these years, you may be able to trace it to your anxiety. Other events you consciously cannot remember, the subconscious does and may play a major role in you having anxiety. Anxiety is the body's way of trying to do what it perceives as protecting you from experiencing an unpleasant event similar from the past again.

The individual I was speaking to explained to me that when he was a child, he went to the bathroom at a birthday party and closed the door. When he closed the door, the door handle fell off. This kept him from opening the door to get out. The bathroom was small and the noise from the party kept anyone from hearing him as he beat on the door and yelled to get out. To his memory, he was in there forever before someone found him and was able to get the door open. He remembers the event like it was yesterday and today as a 30-year-old man, he has anxiety going into a bathroom and locking the door, especially at a small restaurant where the bathroom only fits one person and there is a lot of noise outside.

He has learned to not resist the anxiety, but acknowledge it and focus on the task of going to the restroom. You see, he quit trying to ignore the anxiety, fearing it and trying to make it go away. These thoughts do nothing, but increase and fuel your anxiety. He now learned to acknowledge it, quit fearing it, (he realized he was going to be ok) and started observing it with curiosity like observing the rainstorm from inside your house instead of actually being in it. It's like taking a step back and observing what's going on, versus being *caught up* in what's going on.

I'm going to be completely transparent in hopes this will help someone in my particular situation. My anxiety today results in a lifetime of unremitting stress of not being good enough in all areas of my life. As a child, my mother and I were very poor. She would go to bed some nights without eating, in order to feed me. We literally had nothing and toys were not something I experienced on a regular basis. There was this army soldier at a store that I don't recall the name of, but I wanted it for a long time. It came with a parachute and when you threw it up in the air, the parachute opened and it glided to the ground.

This was $3.00, maybe $4.00, at the most. My mom bought it for me one day with money I'm sure we couldn't afford to spend and I felt like the luckiest kid in the world. The next day, I went to my Nana's house where I spent a lot of my days as a child, to play with the neighborhood kids. I showed them my new plastic army figure that I was so proud of as they all looked on with amazement.

I then threw it up in the air and as the parachute opened, they all were cheering and saying how cool it was. I remember how great I felt. Not that I had something they didn't, but at that moment I was good enough, an equal and accepted. The very next day I was so excited to go to my Nana's to once again bring my $4.00 plastic army man with a parachute to play with the neighborhood kids.

As we all met, one of the boys was overly excited in our group to show us something. He then pulled out a plastic army man with a parachute. He didn't only pull out a plastic army man with a parachute, he pulled out an army man that was three times the size of my army man and a parachute to go with it. He pulled out the army man with a parachute that probably cost $20.00. He threw it up in the air and as the parachute opened; I felt like it was so big, it blocked the sun. Everyone cheered and made comments on how much "cooler" it was than mine. That day broke me.

I went into my Nana's house and broke down crying. I felt completely defeated, worthless and not an equal. I never thought much about it, but I'm sure it made my mom feel the same way. I was too young to give any thought on how that made my mom feel at the time. That event skewed the way I viewed myself forever, along with growing up most of my early childhood poor and doing without. The anxiety started at an early age, I just didn't recognize it as that. Anxiety is fear spread thin.

It can be the fear of past regrets or future unknown. Mine was and always has been, future unknown. In sports, I was a wrestler on a 5A state championship team. The other guys on the team were amazing, yet I was on the same varsity level. Was I good enough to be on this team was the question that occupied my mind all the time? The times I believed I was, I could pretty much beat anyone. My coach Kenny Nelson once told me, "Travis there are days you can win the state championship by the way you wrestle and some days I don't understand what's going on."

The times I doubted it, I could lose to someone not even as skilled as me. After High School, I pursued a bodybuilding career where I won four Mr. Oklahoma titles in my respected weight division. Did I enjoy it? No! The whole process for years was fear-driven. I wasn't interested in winning Mr. Oklahoma titles, I was looking for approval and acceptance to anyone that would give it to me. And although a lot of people see the four Mr. Oklahoma titles, there were some competitions where I placed second. A very respected placing out of several competitors, but to me it was a major defeat. The person that beat me had the $20.00 plastic army man with the giant parachute. Most know me today for my 35 plus years in the fitness industry.

I've been a personal trainer with a private studio making six figures to owning a full-service fitness center. After selling that business, I started Garza's Fat Loss Camps. I started as one location specifically to help overweight people with my patented 5lb dumbbell workouts. Since then, I have grown to six locations, I own in Oklahoma, along with a live online broadcast system that reaches all over the world for those wanting to workout from home. I have six licensed camps in Illinois and Indiana with others pending opening in different states.

My second company is Myosculpt Nutrition, which is my own supplement company where we now ship orders every day to people all over the United States and have a brick and mortar store Garza's Wholesale Sports Nutrition in Edmond, OK for locals to purchase my and other companies supplement line. My third company is SHK Consulting, which is my consulting business for those wanting to open a Garza's Fat Loss Camp locally or in another state. I bring this to your attention not to brag, but to make a point. You may be asking with all this, why does Travis have anxiety?

If anxiety is fear spread thin and about past regret or the future unknown, how does this even remotely affect Travis? What does Travis fear? He has three businesses, a great marriage, three beautiful daughters and a good lifestyle. I fear the answer to the question am I good enough? I fear I am not deserving of this life God has given me. I fear I am never doing a good enough job for God, my family, my clients and my staff. My entire success in business, up until about a year ago, has been solely fear-driven. The part of fear that is the (future unknown).

Fear I would be poor again as I was in my childhood. Fear that someone could be around the corner with a $20.00 plastic army man with a parachute bigger than mine. My fear drove me to do whatever it took to never be poor again. I made sure I was always one step ahead by working day and night making my parachute bigger and bigger. Along with fearing failing in business, I feared letting God down, scared of letting my wife and kids down, feared I was letting my clients down and letting my staff down.

My fear of failing and insecurity of never being good enough for over 35 years, finally caught up to me. Fear spread in this many directions produces years of unremitting stress in the mind and eventually surfaces as anxiety. Simply put, I worried about being good enough. Once anxiety shows up, fear to anxiety is like gasoline on a campfire. The beauty of going through this, is, I now relate more than ever to my target clientele.

The overweight person that doesn't feel accepted, but rather intimidated, scared and alone at other places. How do I relate? The fear I have of failing in business, they have of failing to get their weight under control. The fear I have of not being good enough and deserving of my success, they have of not being good enough because of their weight to have a good relationship, good job, friends and children. For over eight months, I tried to get rid of

20

anxiety. I tried to will it away. I was a guy that had overcome a lot of obstacles in his life and this was no different. Once I educated myself on what anxiety actually is and try to identify what brought this about, I became curious. I wanted to learn about it, so I could better understand it. This approach was a result of my fear dialing way down and I began to build a relationship with it. For me, it was not typically one thing, but worrying about several things. The story from my childhood was only the beginning. The compound effect of everything moving forward caused anxiety to surface.

Start by addressing something that sticks out in your childhood that you have never forgotten. Then think about present-day and what situation your anxiety is triggered the most. Is there a connection like my friend who got locked in the bathroom and today gets triggered by small bathrooms in noisy places? Next, be true to yourself and write down the things in your life you fear the most. Don't just think about them write them down. One by one, you need to address them. Try and connect at what point in your life that became a fear. What event, or events, caused this to become a fear? This is what I mean by building a relationship with anxiety. Breaking it down and understanding what's causing it. We spend so much time fighting it, medicating it and running from it instead of stopping and being present in the moment and acknowledging that it's happening. It also involves you being curious about what just happened, what was said, or what did you see that set your anxiety off? Once you start to write these occurrences down and better understand your anxiety, you will be on the road to a more peaceful and calm life.

I want to address something in regards to medication used for anxiety. I am not a Doctor so this is not medical advice. I'm basing this off of my life experiences and my own findings. There is no shame in being on anxiety medication, as it has a role in helping people with anxiety. I will say this. It's only a band-aid. The medication will mask and keep the anxiety suppressed. Until the underlying cause of your anxiety is addressed, either through professional counseling or self-exploration like I did along with changes in your lifestyle, it will always be there in one format or another. It doesn't go away, but you can successfully manage it.

Anxiety is an emotion you were born with, like everyone else. It may go away temporarily, but when it's triggered, it will resurface. To keep this from happening as little as possible, you want to understand it and genuinely try to build a relationship with it, instead of resisting it. This is your first step on the road to a better life.

CHAPTER 3

Talk About It

Now that you have some understanding of anxiety, I'm hoping your fear has lessened knowing you're not alone and it's an emotion we all have. Let's take the next step and talk about it. That January morning I woke up to a different world that immediately terrified me and my first thought was not to tell anyone about it. I didn't want to share what I was experiencing with anyone because I felt it would cause them to possibly panic, which would add to my already panicking mind. It was such an indescribable feeling and my thoughts were so jumbled, I didn't know how anyone else could make sense of it if I did try and explain it to them. Second, humans tend to internalize those things we feel others will view as something wrong. Third, I thought I needed to remain calm and figure this out on my own, so that I wouldn't cause my wife and family to worry.

I thought to myself, *Travis you have figured out and solved some of the biggest problems that you have come up against in your life and this is the reason you run several businesses with success. Solving problems on a large scale is what you do everyday.* This thinking gave me a sense of comfort, but it didn't last long. Weeks went by and what I was experiencing, (now known as anxiety) was wearing me down. I now couldn't sleep and this added to the severity of the anxiety, which escalated my fear, increased my heart rate and ultimately my blood pressure.

For weeks, I fought this battle and the continuous cycle of no sleep, fear and the unexplainable, increased my heart rate like I was running a marathon with the back of my head feeling like it was going to explode. The body eventually will protect itself. When things get extreme and it cannot physically take anymore, it starts to shut down. One day, I remember waking up on the cold bathroom floor at my headquarters building. I had passed out unknowingly. As I lay there, I could faintly hear my staff laughing down the hall. My first thoughts were, how long had I been out? Did they know something was wrong?

I gathered myself off the floor. As I looked in the mirror, I remembered seeing a reflection of a man that was aging rapidly. I splashed cold water on my face and went back out to the office area to get a feel to see if anyone knew I had fainted or would comment on how long I was in the bathroom. Nothing was said and business went on as usual. I had escaped revealing my secret nightmare, but how long could I keep it up? I made it through the day and the only sense of relief I experienced was when I was driving my car home.

I didn't have to put on an act and I could be alone with my thoughts, which now looking back, was the worst thing I could do. Being alone, even for a short time, gives the mind the opportunity to dial your anxiety up because you're now 100% focused on the anxiety. As much as that relief came, it was gone again as I got closer to my home. I remember each day going through the guard gates into my neighborhood. As soon as I passed through the guard gates, my indescribable situation, (now known as anxiety) would start to escalate. I would walk into my house and put on the act in front of my wife and two-year-old twin daughters, that life was good.

Under normal circumstances, most people would look at being home as a time to see the wife and kids and enjoy time together. My only thought was to hold on until the kids went to bed at 7:30 p.m., and then I could retreat to the bathroom to shower and be alone with my thoughts. Once I had taken a shower, I spent a moment summoning up the courage to go out, face my wife and put on the final act of the day. I only had to put on the act that life was great until 10 p.m., and then I could retreat to bed where even though I was getting no sleep, I didn't have to interact with anyone and I could once again be alone with my thoughts.

The next morning I got up and started the routine all over again. I had it down to an art how many people and situations through the week I would have to be involved with and for approximately how long I would have to put on an act to get through it. On Mondays, I had to put on an act at HeadQuarters meetings for *Garza's Fat Loss Camps* for 10 department managers. Tuesday's act would be for my supplement company meeting with managers at *Garza's Wholesale Sports Nutrition*. Wednesday's big act, would be picking up my 14-year-old daughter Sydney from school and find a way to get through a conversation about her life and helping with it. Weekend struggles were going to soccer games on Saturdays and church on Sundays.

Pre-anxiety, I lived for weekends to watch Sydney play soccer and attend church on Sunday. Now it had become a task to just get through. Everyday had its battle along with keeping it together at home for my wife and twin daughters Koti and Haven. I slowly started getting up each morning, looking at my pillow as I got out of bed thinking to myself, "Just 15 more hours. You can lay back down and not have to put on an act for awhile." This was my life for approximately one month. Get up and exist...alone.

By this time, I had no idea what my wife was thinking, or if she even knew something was wrong. I wasn't concerned anymore if she had caught on yet. I was trying to make it through the day with nothing more than my thoughts. One evening, while in the kitchen, I couldn't do it anymore and walked to the living room where my wife Andrea sat watching one of her shows. I sat down and she looked at me and said, *"What's wrong Travis?"* I then broke down crying and revealed to her everything that had been going on for a couple of months, from the morning it started until now.

I lost track of time and how long we talked, but it seemed like forever. I will never forget after we talked, feeling a sense of relief like I hadn't felt in what seemed like years, come over me. The anxiety was still there, but my fear lowered to a 2 on a scale of 1-10. Knowing that someone knew I was in a bad place and telling them everything, gave me somewhat of a safe feeling. Hearing Adrea say "I love you and we are going to get through this together," allowed me to sleep that night, better than I had in a month. The next step on the road to recovery is to talk about it and pray about it before going to bed each night.

I believe our first instinct is to keep what we are going through to ourselves. Please don't make the BIG mistake I did and do that. I could have knocked off months of my own personal recovery by talking to someone sooner. Isolating yourself is the worst thing you can do to yourself in regards to anxiety. When you go it alone, you're just going to spend more time inside your own head, with your mind racing faster and faster. Your fear begins to rev up and the overall pressure starts to build. Holding it in, will eventually manifest into physical symptoms that will cause most doctors to diagnose you as perfectly healthy. Bottling it up is the last thing you want to do. Talking to someone will help get you out of your own head.

Let someone know you need help. Put your ego aside and let someone in. By not putting my ego aside and not asking for help, I allowed my own thoughts and growing fear to take me to a place that took longer to recover from, than if I would have spoken up that very first day when I woke up in a different world. After my two years of research and study, I found one consistent commonality - talking about anxiety immediately lowers it. I experienced this first hand even after keeping it bottled up for one month, the night I broke down and told my wife.

In order for this to truly work, you need to find the right person to talk to. You will need to find a person that truly cares about you and will listen to you talk about your situation possibly every day. When anxiety is first experienced, most are scared. Not of any thing in particular, but a constant feeling of fear. As I stated earlier, anxiety is fear spread thin. I think my wife would tell you I talked about it constantly. When I was revved up, it felt good to talk to her about it and try and make sense of it. When I got home from work, I couldn't help but talk about it. The person you choose has to truly care about you, have patience and understand that talking about it, is part of the recovery process.

Talking about it gives you a sense of not being alone and safe. To some people who have not gone through, or ever experienced anxiety, a person talking about what they are going through all the time, may cause them to purposely avoid you. That's ok. Don't be offended by it. They care about you, they just don't understand how you feel and unless they experience it, they never will.

Some people will truly care about you, but are not cut out to listen on a daily basis or discuss the same topic over and over again. It's like me and blood. If you cut your arm open, I truly care about you getting help, but I will be the first one to walk away. I'm not cut out to see blood and will pass out if I do. I care, I'm just not the right person to help. There is that one person that truly wants to help you, just by listening to your story everyday. They are cut out to listen to you everyday if that's what you need to feel better. They want to talk to you about it if you need them to with a genuine interest. They're out there, you just have to look around.

It could be your mom, dad, sister, spouse, best friend or co-worker. In some circumstances, you may have to find a counselor who specializes in this. I found, (for me) someone who actually knows me. In my case, my wife works best. I would advise waiting to talk to someone that is actually experiencing anxiety at the same time you are. It seems logical to share with people that are in the same situation you are and for some that's true. Be careful not to get stuck with it being ok that everyday feels like the worst day of your life. Some people are ok with staying in that place and talking about it.

I want much more for you and I'm living proof you can co-exist and actually form a good relationship with anxiety and have a normal life. You have to apply the tools I'm giving you in this book on a regular basis. I am a believer in Jesus Christ and that He died on the cross for us. God's Word says we were created for, "connection" not created to be alone. Not created to drift towards isolation. This is for all things, not just in intimate relationships. Connection in all we do, including all that we suffer. While you look for that right person to talk to, I want to let you know this. Jesus is right by your side. He walks with you everyday in all that you do. He promises to never leave your side.

I can tell you there were times I didn't want to believe this because I felt so alone. But I look back and realize all the things He helped me get through. At some moments, I have no idea how I accomplished some of the things I did it in the condition I was in for over eight months. The things I accomplished and can barely remember during that eight months, was simply Jesus carrying me when I couldn't walk. There were nights I went to bed asking God why I was going through this? What did I do to deserve it? Yet, I still found myself praying for tomorrow to be a better day.

I want you right now to put this book down and find someone to talk to about your situation. Don't read the next chapter until you have done this. It may take you going through one to three people to find the right one, but this is a very important step before moving on. Whether you believe in Jesus or not, before you go to sleep, pray to receive peace, give thanks for the good things in your life and to have a better day tomorrow.

Last, I want you to know this, while you are looking for that person to talk to. I understand you. I know exactly how you're feeling and I truly care about you. I also know it's going to get better for you and you're going to be ok. Now go find that person to talk about it...please.

CHAPTER 4

Get Your Values In Order

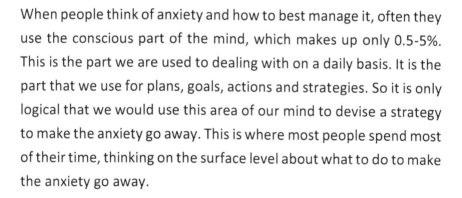

When people think of anxiety and how to best manage it, often they use the conscious part of the mind, which makes up only 0.5-5%. This is the part we are used to dealing with on a daily basis. It is the part that we use for plans, goals, actions and strategies. So it is only logical that we would use this area of our mind to devise a strategy to make the anxiety go away. This is where most people spend most of their time, thinking on the surface level about what to do to make the anxiety go away.

We consume our thoughts leaving no stone unturned for a solution to our anxiety. The one area very few have knowledge of, which contributes to people having anxiety are values, which are buried in the subconscious. More importantly, the question to be asked is are your values in alignment with the way you are living? The subconscious has been programmed from early childhood on what we value. Your values can make up things like your belief/religion, how you view relationships, your work ethic and overall view of life.

Living your life in accordance to your values brings peace in the mind. To put it another way, your conscious mind commands and your subconscious mind obeys. Your subconscious mind is an unquestioning servant. It works day and night to make your behavior fit a pattern consistent with your emotionalized thoughts, hopes and desires. Your subconscious mind grows either flowers or weeds in the garden of your life. In this chapter, I'm going to ask you to sit down and get real with yourself. By not living your life according to your values, you are creating ongoing stress in the back of your mind, that you are not even aware is going on.

The subconscious is trying to make it fit in, but the values don't match up; thus you have what I call an underlying issue that you're not consciously aware of. I compare it to leaving the house and knowing you forgot something, but can't quite put your finger on it. You may be going through life and consciously thinking everything is good, but feel like something is wrong. You search for it on the surface and check all the boxes, but nothing comes to mind. Let me give you an example of one of my values that I never thought was an issue because I had a good excuse for not doing it.

When my twins were born, you can only imagine the endless nights of zero sleep on top of running three businesses. I have always had a rule without exception, that I go to church and give God His day by praising Him. I was brought up this way from birth and have lived my entire life like this. I never missed church and I truly love going. When people would ask why I love going to church, I would tell them it was like a drug I needed each week, applying the message to my own life to help me start the week off being a better person.

If I missed, due to being sick or out of town, my week was never as good as the Sundays I attended. I use this example to show that even some things out of your control can go against your values and cause unidentified anxiety. My twins were newborns and we were always exhausted, so church became a hit and miss for me and my wife, with more miss than hit. What I so deeply cherished was being misaligned by my actions and was causing stress to accumulate in my subconscious.

When several things in your life are misaligned with your values, stress begins to accumulate and eventually can surface as anxiety. In my profession at Garza's Fat Loss Camps, I see misalignment all the time. One reason I believe this is the case is because a lot of my clients have anxiety. Misalignment is when you want one thing, but do the opposite or chase something else. My clients come to Garza's wanting to lose weight and (value) being healthy, being able to play with their kids, participate in activities overweight people typically cannot do and they want to sleep better.

It's fair to say, they have valued these things for a big portion of their life, but some find themselves doing things that go against these values such as over eating, not exercising, not getting adequate sleep, and possibly drinking to much. These are misalignments most people can identify with, on one level or another. I want to look and feel great, yet my actions are keeping me from experiencing what I desire. I feel this particular misalignment between actions and goals causes more stress, frustration and failure in the society of an overweight population than anything else.

It's a misalignment that a lot of people have lived with from childhood into their adult life. So while some misalignments may be temporary, like the example I used in regards to me going to church, this misalignment has been going on for a lifetime for a significant portion of our population. Wanting to be healthy is not enough. Our actions must line up with our goals. Over my 35 plus years in the fitness industry, I have received e-mails, testimonies and witnessed thousands of my clients that go through my program stating they no longer have anxiety, are off anxiety medication, or can manage their anxiety and have a normal, happy life. When realignment with their value of being healthy matches up with their actions, they reduced their stress, which reduces anxiety.

I want to address a cause of anxiety in the world we live in today that is growing rapidly particularly, due to social media. It's called *comparison syndrome.* This is when you compare yourself to other people in many ways such as their body shape, their house, their car, their spouse, or maybe even the job they have. There are a number of different things that people compare themselves to, to determine if they are successful, living the good life and where they should be. Basically, it's when you compare yourself to other people and start to believe you need to do what they are doing, have what they have and be more like who they are.

When we view other people's lives as better than ours and we start to change our actions to align with someone else's values (not ours), we start to feel stressed. These are not your values. I'm as guilty as anyone of this. I spent years being told to always find someone doing better than you are and pattern your life after theirs. This holds true to some extent, until you start taking it to an unhealthy level. I have always had a mentor or coach most of my career. I feel everyone needs a coach in an area of life you want to succeed in. The mentors I have had throughout the years, are all great and I highly respect each of them.

I would meet with my mentors every three months to go over strategies to help Garza's Fat Loss Camps to be better at helping change people's lives. For several years we would meet, I got ideas, and I went back home and implemented them. I'm not sure when the change started, but it was gradual at first. I didn't even realize it had taken place until I started my journey seeking the cause of my anxiety. I realized I had taken on the personality of some of my mentors. To be perfectly clear, their personalities and beliefs are not bad in anyway at all...they were not mine.

I had built such a great friendship with them, that somewhere I decided I wanted to be like them. To be completely transparent, I never had a father figure in my life. I was raised by two amazing and strong women, my mother and my NaNa. Subconsciously, as a boy without a father, I probably had been looking my whole life for a male figure I could identify with, that was on a higher playing field, (like boys view their fathers) than me.

I've gone through my whole life fear-driven to be the best and I've always questioned if the way I'm living my life is the best I can do? Can I do better? Am I a good enough father to my kids? By starting to take on the traits of someone else, it immediately starts the misalignment of who you truly are. Looking back, I was treating my wife, mom and kids differently. Not in an abusive way, but putting my work first and them second. I thought that in order to be more successful, this is what I needed to do.

I didn't realize it, but subconsciously this was a ticking time bomb waiting to go off in the form of anxiety because subconsciously the resistance was going on for years. And on that January morning, the ticking time bomb went off. Over the course of the past year when I was told at the heart hospital I have anxiety, my life changed. One big change I made after discovering my values and misalignments, was to be who I truly am for the first time in my life, to quit operating out of fear and operate out of what defines happiness to me. That is being with my wife more. Talking to my mom each day. Taking the time out to make my kids breakfast and their lunches every day, and give them a bath every night. To be there for my 15-year-old Sydney during her teenage years and on. Being present in the moment with each of them and not thinking ahead all the time about what I need to do with my three businesses. Does this cut into my workday and time I could be growing my businesses at a faster rate? I said yes at first when I made a conscious decision to make these changes, but it would align with what I truly value.

The reality is it actually was the opposite. By truly being myself, spending time with my family and kids and getting rid of the (underlying guilt) that came with me not doing it, my business has taken on a new success in many ways I never thought possible. I work less, but think so much clearer, smarter, faster and happier doing it more than ever. I'm laser-focused on my work when I'm at work and truly present with my wife and kids when I'm home and not going through the motions. I now take Thursdays off to be with my wife and have a date night.

Do times come up when I feel I should be working or doing more? Of course, but I immediately think about the peace I have found living my life aligned with my values. Now I want you to get real with yourself. Take a notepad and go somewhere you will not be disturbed and not rushed for time. I want you to start by identifying your values. Some things will surface immediately and some will require some thought. Take your time and really think about what's important to you and gives you some peace just thinking about it. You may find things that you value and call your name, will interfere with your goal if you were to truly align those values with your actions. Ask yourself if the goal is worth the anxiety it's causing by the misalignment of what you truly value?

Also note that values will start to surface as you become more focused on finding them. So if you only come up with one or two initially, it's ok. More will start to surface as you start to become aware of what causes your anxiety to go up. Now that you have written down your values, I want you to become aware of the activities and habits that are not in line with these values. Write those down. Next, I want you to write down what actions you're going to put in place to replace the habits that are not in alignment with your values.

This written task will begin to reduce your anxiety. This is a discovery process that unfolds as you start to direct your attention specifically to finding your values. So many people are going through life and acting in ways they don't really want to, but they feel life demands or requires it. I know people that go out drinking with their friends weekly that truly don't want to do it, but feel it's what they should do to be social.

I want to tell you to quit looking around at our society's definition of what happiness is and find yourself, your values and what gives you peace. Live your best life, whatever that may be and when the day comes to leave this earth, you can look back with a smile on your face and have no regret of what you wish you would have valued. I thank God for that January morning I woke up with anxiety, believe it or not because that's what it took for me to find what I truly value.

I've cried many times over the thought of continuing my quest to act like someone I wasn't at the expense of putting my family second. The thought of waking up one day knowing I had missed out on all those memories, time with my kids, talks with my mom, date nights with my wife all for more success. Go now and find your values, align them with your actions and make adjustments to your life to find the true meaning of peace and happiness.

CHAPTER 5

Putting Structure In Place

Creating space in the mind is one of the ways to focus and reduce anxiety. In the last chapter we placed your values in order and aligned them with your actions. This creates space in the mind, when you take away the resistance that was there due to the misalignment. The more space we create, the more the effects of anxiety decrease. Now, let's move into an area of your life that you may not be aware of that causes anxiety, lack of structure.

Not having structure in your life can be causing you anxiety. Although all of our days are unique in the tasks we perform, I want to show you a few we can all relate to. What if your day begins with getting up late? It immediately puts you in panic mode to get ready for work. You try and eat something, but most likely skip breakfast due to being in a hurry. Driving to work is stressful because you're now in a hurry. We don't want to be late and get frustrated at the traffic that is "causing us to be late." You arrive to work stressed out and this sets the tone for your day. You grab whatever for lunch or skip it, so you can catch up on your social media.

After work, you think about getting a workout in, but wind up skipping it altogether since your day was so stressful, but reassuring yourself you will get one in tomorrow. You arrive home feeling completely exhausted and possibly have a drink to try and make it all better. You end the day staying up late watching Netflix and eating dinner that isn't the best choice. You go to bed late and start the cycle the next day all over again. I call this day being active without accomplishment.

If you are always in activity mode (busy), but never getting anything done you start to feel like your not accomplishing anything. When we remain stuck in this cycle of feeling unaccomplished, this causes stress, which eventually will surface as anxiety. The answer to an anxiety ridden life is structure. With structure comes the feeling of being accomplished because we get things done that are of value to us. When you have more structure in your life, you create more space in the mind, which leads to a quieter mind.

If you have children, you probably created a structured day for them. What time they get up, eat, nap and go to bed. It's proven that kids like structure and thrive better in a structured environment. What you may not know is so do adults. It's also proven that adults who live a life of structure are happier, less stressed, more productive and more successful in accomplishing their goals. When you have a structure in place, the mind isn't constantly problem-solving in all areas of your life. Putting structure in place in areas of our life you **can control** creates space in the mind so we can solve problems calmly that arise in our life and are out of our control.

The more areas in your life you can create structure, the lower your anxiety will be. There is a rule to putting structure in place that must be used if you want to work towards an anxiety free life. That rule is: Do not allow anyone to cause you to deviate from your structure. Structure is no good for your anxiety if you cannot stick to it because you are around people that don't respect it.

The first step is to sit down and list the things you can control. Note: When creating a list of things you can control and put structure in place, try and pick those things you know will not affect anyone in your household. This way you will have little, or no resistance, from anyone, which in return gives you peace of mind in itself. Then list the things you know **you cannot control** and put structure in place. This inadvertently gives you a sense of peace. Knowing it's out of your control allows you to let it go. I am going to give you the three pillars I use on myself and my clients to reduce anxiety.

These three pillars are within your control and should be done each day at the same time or as close as possible. These three pillars have been proven to lower anxiety in the medical field. You will need to sit down and list the time of day you will complete each to insure they don't clash with some of your other tasks including tasks that involve your children or spouse. This will take away the possibility of someone trying to deviate you from your new structure. The first pillar is eating for a calm mind.

Structuring the time you eat your meals every day relieves the mind of the stress of solving the problem of when you will get to your next meal. Less stress, less anxiety. The foods you eat dictate the intensity of your anxiety in two ways. The first is, the food can cause anxiety to elevate. Let me be clear about something. I'm not going to give you a list of magical foods that get rid of anxiety. The key is to stabilize blood sugar, which is what I do with my clients through my eating plans to help them lose weight.

The same approach to help my clients lose weight by stabilizing blood sugar also helps to reduce their anxiety. Having your blood sugar stabilized, means you're not having ups and downs mentally. Eating junk food, which is loaded with sugar, causes your blood sugar to rise along with anxiety. When the sugar burns off, you crash and maybe feeling low. This up and down roller coaster can cause anxiety to spin out of control. Eating four to five small meals per day of good food, will help stabilize blood sugar leaving you with less anxiety and feeling good.

The meals should consist of a lean protein such as eggs, chicken, turkey, ham, or fish. Starchy carbs such as sweet potato, rice (brown or white), oatmeal, Rye bread, beans, or fruit. And a fibrous carb such as carrots, zucchini, salad greens, or green beans. The simple way to know how much to eat without measuring is to put some of each, (protein, starchy carbs, and fibrous carbs) on a plate in equal portions. Use the protein such as chicken breast to set the standard of portions on the plate. Eat some of each until you're full, not stuffed.

Spread your 4-5 meals out approximately 3-4 hours apart from each other. Removing sugar, caffeine and alcohol from my diet has been a big contributor to lowering my anxiety. Drinking alcohol and sugar were not my main vices, but caffeine was. Caffeine, I learned through my studies, actually will mask anxiety for a long time. It can go undetected until the anxiety reaches a boiling point and surfaces. Caffeine will intensify your anxiety without a doubt. Learning to live a life caffeine free was hard at first, but now my life is so much more peaceful without it and that's what I want for you.

The second part is the mental aspect of what you eat that so many people overlook. I believe people instinctively want to eat healthy. When we go against that instinct, we cause resistance in the mind, which leads to anxiety. We are misaligned with our value of eating good and the action we are taking. People tend to self-medicate with bad food excessively and find themselves satisfied in the moment only to wake up the next day hating themselves for eating it. When we eat good food, we feel a sense of accomplishment, which leads to serotonin release in the brain, which makes us feel good and lowers anxiety.

Food is as powerful as drugs. The second pillar is (morning) workouts. Pre-Anxiety, I would wake up each day and immediately start thinking about when I could squeeze a workout in. Sometimes, if I had an hour to spare in the afternoon, I would go workout and then if the day ran late, I would stop at my community gym in the development I live in to workout. Everyday was a guessing game.

Working out had been my whole life since the age of 18. I had competed for many years in bodybuilding shows and my entire career revolved around working out. Working out was high on my list of values. Although I seemed to find time to get a workout in, deep down I knew the workouts were meaningless. My mind was always on what I had to do next and not truly enjoying what I love.

The resistance in my mind between my value of working out and the actions I was taking of having meaningless work-outs at random times was causing stress, which contributed to my anxiety eventually surfacing. It's no secret in modern day science, that exercise has proven to be beneficial in reducing and offsetting many health-related problems. One of the most studied is exercise related to lowering anxiety. It's scientifically proven that exercise on a regular basis, reduces anxiety.

Exercise does not have to be an everyday task or at an extreme level, like some people think. When I was first diagnosed with anxiety, the thought of exercise was the last thing on my mind because of how bad my anxiety was and how bad I felt. I felt so bad I didn't work out for a few months until my mother said to me one day, "You feel like crap anyway, so you might as well go workout." Those words were the best thing anyone could have said to me at that time.

I knew the benefits of working out in the reduction of anxiety from my years of being in the fitness industry, yet I was paralyzed by what I was going through. I started out very slow and for a short amount of time. It was very hard for me. A person who had worked out for years at a high level to humble himself and start out very slow. Working out stresses the body and too much stress on the body, will increase anxiety the same way as to much stress on the mind, will increase anxiety. This is not to scare you or keep you from working out. This is to inform you that working out is a vague word and can be interpreted in many ways.

If your anxiety is extreme like mine was, start out slow and in short sessions. Don't feel like it's a waste of your time if you only workout

10 minutes because that's all you can handle at the time. I was there and it gets better. Then, after your body adapts to the 10 minutes, add five more. It's a process, but it will work for you. To be transparent, I work out Monday, Wednesday, and Friday for one hour. Although it's not the workouts I used to do, it has now become something I look forward to again and feel great about myself. When we exercise, it causes serotonin, the feel good hormone, to release, which in return causes the symptoms of anxiety to lessen.

Exercise reduces stress, which is the main cause for anxiety to surface. Exercise, like eating good food, leaves you with the feeling of accomplishment. When we feel accomplished, we feel good about ourselves. I wanted to address when to workout last because of the many reasons behind my answer. Remember, we are creating a structure in your life, so your mind can get these tasks off its plate of problems to solve for the day. Through my own experience, I have found working out in the morning before my kids and wife are up, gives me a peace of mind for so many reasons.

First, I don't feel rushed or anxious and it's completely 100% my time to better myself through exercise. There is something so peaceful about getting up when most of the world is asleep. You're not having to answer questions or deal with problems. It's quiet. I'm also starting my day off doing something positive and that sets the tone for the day. Most people get up when they have to or late in panic mode with the world and its problems right there in their face. They haven't had time to adjust and prepare their mind for the day. Getting up early and working out prepares you mentally for the day with a peaceful mind. I feel accomplished before even starting my day after I workout. My actions are aligned with my value of working out and it's off my mind's plate of problems to solve, which creates space in my mind.

At first, you will battle with wanting to get that extra hour of sleep versus getting up and working out. The third pillar will help you with this. Once you experience the peace and reduction of anxiety by getting up early and working out, you will never question if you should get up early and workout. I want to give you a gift to help get you started on your way to reducing your anxiety with an eating and workout plan, designed by myself. The best part is you do it from the **comfort of your own home** and I'm giving you the first (2-weeks) FREE for you to see if it's a fit for you.

The comforting part about doing my program from home, is anxiety can increase with just the thought of going out in public places, especially to workout. People in general tend to be self- conscious of others watching them work out. My workout system only requires the use of 5lb dumbbells, done from your home, and are 40 minutes long. As I stated earlier, start out with only 5-10 minutes if that's all you can do and work your way up from there.

The workouts are a LIVE broadcast from one of my camp locations and a trainer will be guiding you every step of the way from saying hello to you to demonstrate each exercise before actually doing it. The eating plan is super easy to follow and will start you on your way to stabilizing blood sugar. To get started go to www.athomelivetransformation.com and register for your FREE two weeks. Once you register, we will call you and welcome you along with answering any questions you have and getting you ready for your first workout. 😊

The third and final pillar is one that many people overlook with anxiety and would never think plays a major role in it. The third pillar is discipline in sleeping. Going to bed at a specific, structured time and getting up at a specific, structured time lowers anxiety. I was guilty of working long days and then staying up late as a way to justify having some kind of home life. Some nights, I would go to bed at 10:00 p.m. other nights, 12:30 a.m. There was never a set time for bed. I would wake up in the morning based on when I heard one of my twin girls cry and that time could vary from 6:00 a.m. - 7:00 a.m.

This kind of non-structure of when to go to sleep and when to wake up, keeps the mind in a problem-solving mode of when to fall asleep and when to wake up. This causes the mind to be restless from trying to constantly adapt to a non-structured sleeping and waking time. When I started studying the effects of a structured sleeping schedule and its effects on lowering anxiety, it made all the sense in the world. We put our children on structured sleeping schedules for a reason.

When a child stays up past their bedtime or miss their nap, it's very noticeable. They are irritable, cry over the smallest things and seem more irrational. When they are put to bed on a scheduled time, nap at a certain time, and get up each morning at a certain time, you have a pleasant rational kid a majority of the time. Why is it that as we become adults, we feel this is not applicable to us anymore? I would say it's even more applicable to us as adults as we are dealing with the stress of life and its problems. When you add a non structured bed and wake time to an already stressful life, you start to create the perfect setting for anxiety to surface. I was determined to use every tool I read about and now giving you, to fight my anxiety including a scheduled sleep and wake time each day including weekends.

I set my sleep time for 10:00 p.m. and my wake time 5:00 a.m. and was not going to let anyone deviate me from this. These times do not interfere with my responsibilities as a husband or father. It was hard at first, making myself go to bed at 10:00 pm. If a game was on, or a movie, I had to push record to stick to my structure. Then set an alarm on my phone for 5:00 a.m. and mentally making myself get up was also a struggle at first.

The big picture behind this is once again creating more space in the mind. The more space you create, the more peaceful your life becomes. Your mind, after about a month of doing this, starts to relax and quits trying to solve the problem of when you go to bed so it can start the shut down of the mind to sleep mode and when you wake up. The mind actually takes it off the plate of problem-solving and fully adapts to the scheduled times. If you're like me and had a hard time falling asleep, this will be a game changer.

The mind actually starts shutting down on its own so to speak at the time you consistently schedule as bed time. It makes falling asleep so much easier and it starts waking up most of the time five minutes before your alarm goes off. You may ask why do I do this on the weekends also? It makes that much of a difference in reducing my anxiety to stay on the schedule seven days a week. The reason we sleep in on the weekends is to catch up on sleep. With this structure, you are rested a majority of the time. Try and set your schedule where you get at least seven hours of sleep, six minimum. Plus on the weekends, getting up a 5:00 a.m. is very peaceful and rewarding. I have the house to myself and can be fully aware and present in the moment, when everyone else gets up instead of waking up out of a dead sleep and just going through the motions with my wife and kids. By instilling this structure, it again brings on a feeling of accomplishment to add to the others. I hope by now you can see where all of this is going.

To create space in the mind by structuring all the things you can control and then being able to use that new space to handle the things you cannot control is an excellent way to live. When there is no space left in the mind, anxiety surfaces. These three pillars I chose for you to put in place are at the top of my list of things to help reduce anxiety. I know most people can put these three pillars in place regardless of what your life consists of. I don't want you to stop with these three. I want you to sit down and write down all the things in your life that you have control of. Then put a structure in place for each of them. It gets easier the more you work on it. Once you start to see the benefits from it, you will be like me constantly looking for what else you can structure in order to create more space in the mind.

6

Meditation (But I'm Not Buddhist)

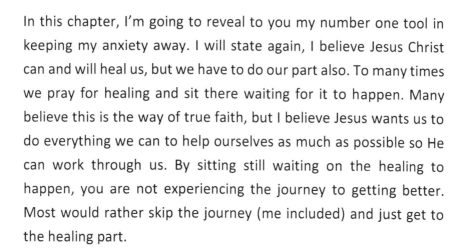

In this chapter, I'm going to reveal to you my number one tool in keeping my anxiety away. I will state again, I believe Jesus Christ can and will heal us, but we have to do our part also. To many times we pray for healing and sit there waiting for it to happen. Many believe this is the way of true faith, but I believe Jesus wants us to do everything we can to help ourselves as much as possible so He can work through us. By sitting still waiting on the healing to happen, you are not experiencing the journey to getting better. Most would rather skip the journey (me included) and just get to the healing part.

The journey is necessary so you can help someone else relate to your experience by connecting with you on a worldly level. By praying to Jesus, we connect with Him on a spiritual level and the two combined are powerful. My number one tool on a worldly level became the practice of meditation. My number one tool on a spiritual level was praying to Jesus for healing. Both, to this day are done on a daily basis. When I was in the Heart Hospital and my time there was coming to an end, I met a man I never would have thought would have made such an impact on my life named Chris Duroy, Ph.D. The Heart Hospital I assumed sent him in to evaluate me and to help determine my frame of mind.

He asked a series of questions that led up to how I felt about what happened. He was referring to me dying for that short period of time. He focused on the after effects of the event that psychologically could have an impact on me. As time went on, I feel we both were enjoying each other's conversation and talked about some of the same people we knew from years past. He then took the conversation in a different direction. He started off by saying, "You are not depressed." You do in fact have anxiety. He stated that as we talked and he brought up certain topics, my heart rate monitor would go through the roof and then when we discussed topics that were non-stressful to talk about, the heart rate monitor would go down. I told him I was not aware that any of our conversation was causing an increase or decrease in my heart rate. That was my first lesson of how powerful the subconscious is. Your conscious mind commands and your subconscious mind obeys. Your subconscious mind is an **unquestioning servant**. Simply put, your subconscious is always problem-solving for you based on your conscious thoughts.

When we are not present or aware of our thoughts and moving through them at a fast pace, anxiety arises in an up and down format. Some topics cause anxiety and some don't. Duroy was monitoring our conversation and could visibly see that several topics caused my anxiety to go up by watching my heart monitor. Everyone has topics that causes their heart rate to increase thus causing stress. For example, you get in a fight with your spouse which causes your heart rate and stress to go up. Until the fight is resolved, the stress level may stay up and may intensify when you are in the same room with them. Once the fight is over, the stress level goes down and the subconscious no longer has a problem to solve and you're in balance once again.

When your subconscious is overloaded with multiple problems to solve on a regular basis, this causes a lot of undetected stress internally and eventually leads to anxiety. Duroy told me the anxiety would only get worse, if I didn't make some changes in my life. He stated some common knowledge things, such as taking some time to myself like a day off, should be the first thing on my agenda to change. Although I only work Monday-Friday he stated with having two-year-old twins, you are working seven days per week, never having time to decompress and do absolutely nothing. Doing nothing was not in my type A personality and would be hard to do, but I was willing to try it.

He stated that eating a healthy diet and working out was a big factor in helping people with anxiety, but was aware that I was already doing that. It made me feel like I was a little ahead of the game to recovery. What he said next made me laugh. He said you need to start meditating. I quickly responded with my shallow un educated brain at the time with, "I'm not Buddhist that's out of the question." He explained to me the act of meditation does not mean you're Buddhist. He gave me a simple task of spending five minutes a day in a quiet place counting my breaths up to 10 and then repeat until my phone alarm went off after five minutes. Breathe in would be 1, out would be 2, in would be 3 and continue on until you reach 10 then start over with 1.

I will admit it was a very hard task for me to sit still and breathe in and out for five minutes in the dark. I found myself more focused on how much time was left until the five minutes were up and I could move on to the things I needed to get done than counting the breaths I was taking. I went through the motions for awhile and then started skipping a day, a week, and eventually, I quit it all together. As I started reading book after book and listening to audio after audio on anxiety, they all had different opinions on how to deal with anxiety, but they all had one thing in common. The practice of meditation. The more I started reading and focusing on this practice, the more I became aware of how many people were actually already doing it and experiencing the benefits from it including getting their anxiety under control.

I want to be completely transparent with you. Learning to meditate and truly understand what meditating is about took me six months to truly start experiencing the benefits from it. Once I started to meditate again daily, I made myself a promise to make it part of my morning routine when everyone else was asleep and never miss. What did I have to lose by changing my mindset from, "I will give it a shot" to "I will accept meditation as a part of my life and let go of the resistance that it's a waste of time?' To truly lean in to the unknown and put away all the stereotypes I had formed about meditation. During my second attempt to start meditating, I actually feared that by meditating, I would wake up one day and be

Buddhist and not even know it. I can't say why I feared being Buddhist except I had formed a stereotype, which is what uneducated people like me do. One of my favorite things I read was, "Buddha was asked: What have you gained from Meditation?" He replied: "Nothing." "However," Buddha said, "Let me tell you what I lost: Anger, Anxiety, Depression, Insecurity, Fear of Old Age, and Death." I read that statement during the peak of my anxiety and it gave me so much comfort I made it the screensaver on my phone. Today, after extensive studies, I feel the Western civilization could learn a lot from the Eastern civilization, in regards to living a more peaceful and happy life through daily meditation without fearing having to change religious beliefs.

To start my new focus on meditation, I was determined to learn everything I could about it. Every technique, the best time to do it, what the atmosphere to mediate should be and how to get the most out of it. The first thing I did was attend an actual meditation class in person. It was a little difficult to find a meditation group as most were tied into a yoga session. I was then told the local VA had them and there was no cost to attend. I found it odd, that the VA was having free meditation sessions, but didn't question it and signed up. My sister Bea Jaye came with me to see what it was all about.

Once I entered the room, I noticed everyone was a military veteran except me and my sister. The experience was definitely out of my comfort zone, but by the time the session had ended, I noticed I was slightly more at ease than normal. I later researched and found that P.T.S.D. (Post Traumatic Stress Disorder) was drastically reduced in ex-military personnel who practice meditation on a regular basis. This finding actually fueled me to dive more into meditation.

Our military are exposed to things I'm sure neither you nor I could ever relate to. This exposure causes the highest level of anxiety (P.T.S.D.). Although I considered my anxiety off the chart, I would never put it in the same category as those with (P.T.S.D.). I will say that my good friend Dr. Bruce Daniels who has been with me through all of this, said, "Travis, what I see you going through is happening more and more as the years go by, look it at like having (Mini P.T.S.D.) due to unremitting stress." I knew at that moment I was on the right track to implementing meditation into my life with full focus.

I want you to understand what meditating does so you can let it work for you. **Meditation teaches you to build a relationship with anxiety. To be curious about it and observe it. To acknowledge it when it arises and not resist it**. Building a relationship with something you don't like, takes work and acceptance. You have to quit looking at anxiety with fear and view it as an emotion that we all have and share. Let that sink in. Everyone around you has some form of anxiety. It's a shared human experience, which means you are not alone. Anxiety shows up when certain things in our environment seem to be a threat to us. With practice when anxiety shows up we want to say to ourselves, "Oh yeah that's anxiety" and then pause and ask yourself is the environment im in at this moment a threat to me? If the answer is no you have to acknowledge this by speaking it. Over time, the majority of the answers to this question will be no and you will start to rebuild a new neural pathway from everything in my environment is a threat, to everything in my environment for the most part is safe. You are now on your way to building a relationship with anxiety by acknowledging it when it arises and addressing it. To be curious and observe anxiety is better explained like this. If you are out in a rainstorm with high winds and crashing lightning, you are actually caught up in and experiencing the rainstorm. If you are inside your house looking out of your window at the same storm, you are observing it and curious about it. If you will start being curious about anxiety when it arises and observing how it makes you feel, you will take yourself out of the loop of fear, irrational thoughts and the physical aspects of anxiety. You start to observe it like a bystander. I stop what I'm doing when my anxiety starts to rise and acknowledge it. I don't pretend it's not happening. I observe that it makes my shoulders tense and become curious if I'm trembling a little or alot. These are two things I personally experience when my anxiety arises that I now observe and not fear.

Once I have fully acknowledged it, I go back to being present in the moment of what I'm doing. This takes all the power away from the emotion (anxiety) and you experience a lesser version of anxiety as you practice this over time. By our natural born instinct's we try to resist unpleasant emotions or block them out. When we try and resist the emotion of anxiety it actually makes it worse. It's like putting gas on a fire. Resisting it makes it worse because you're focused on the anxiety itself in the resistance.

Meditation teaches you to look at anxiety from a whole new perspective, namely Mindfulness. This perspective will be completely opposite of what your logical mind tells you to do in regards to unpleasant emotions. Your logical mind tells you to avoid or escape from the unpleasant feeling. Mindfulness is about being conscious and present in the moment of what you're doing. This took some time for me to understand, but it's basically to be focused on what you're doing at that moment, not lost in thought or worrying about what you need to do or preparing several scenarios for the outcome of some future event that is going to take place.

Being mindful can be as simple as being aware, when you sit down and get up. When you reach for a pen and pick it up. I know it sounds easy, but it's not. These are some of the things we do on autopilot without even thinking about them. Have you ever stopped and asked yourself if you shut the garage door when you came into the house and had to go back to make sure you did? That's a perfect example of not being present. We are always playing a movie in our head about the future or rewinding to the past. Rarely, are we living in the moment.

When we are present in the moment of what we are doing, our subconscious is not in overdrive, problem- solving with what you are thinking about in regards to the future or the past. By doing this, you are creating space in the mind. The more space we create in the mind through meditation, the less the anxiety occurs and the more peaceful we feel. Meditation is not a practice to rid you of anxiety. I know you wanted to hear that, but it's impossible. Anxiety is an emotion such as happy, sad, or mad.

Building a relationship with it takes away the fear and worry. So if being present in the moment is the key to helping anxiety, what is it we do when we meditate? The answer is focus on the breath. I know it sounds a little strange, but stay with me. Don't get caught up like I did trying to figure out the reason for focusing on the breath. There is no reason. It now makes sense to me after meditating for over a year now, so let me save you some time by explaining it so you can reap the benefits faster than I did.

When we focus on the breath, we have one thing to do. Observe our body as we breathe in and the chest rises and when we breathe out and the chest deflates. When I first started, I thought I would have to take big deep breathes in and out, to notice this rise and fall of the chest, but that is not the case. At first, you will take in some deep breaths to start, but a majority of your session, you sit quietly and observe the feeling and sensation of the breath as you inhale and exhale normally. You will start to be curious where you feel the sensation of the breath in the body. Most feel it in the rise and fall of the chest and some feel it in their stomach.

There is no right or wrong way to meditate in this regard. During meditation, your mind will naturally wander away from the focus on the breath. Once you recognize your thoughts have wandered, you simply pause and acknowledge whatever thought you were thinking and then return to focusing on the breath. The reason we practice this, is to train the mind to go into our daily life and learn to be focused solely on the task we are doing at the moment, just like we focus on the breath when we meditate. The way we normally operate is, while we are doing a task we allow our mind to drift in fifty directions trying to solve problems not related to the task being performed. This is called (not being present). Over a period of time, the space in the mind fills up and once it overflows, anxiety typically will surface. It's like a glass of water. If you continue to fill it up and don't stop, it will eventually overflow and make a mess.

It's not that you are never to think about the future or the past again. It's about going there briefly and then returning and being present doing the task you are doing at that moment. So often we go to the future or the past and stay there. By being present in the moment you begin to experience feelings of calm, peace, and enjoying what's actually going on in your life at that moment. Once I started doing this over a period of time, I started experiencing a feeling I can't describe, but pure enjoyment. I spent too many years and time worrying about the future and beating myself up about my past.

I can honestly say until I started being present in the moment, I never realized what I had been missing. Simply put, I was missing life. Life that was going on right now. Not tomorrow or some wish of a different past, but right now in front of me. I noticed more things around me that I took for granted, than ever before. I see things that were meaningless to me like the trees and how they move in the wind, the sun coming up in the morning when I'm done working out, and how much my dogs love me. My wife and kids were always on my radar, but being present in the moment with them in the morning while making their breakfast, instead of worrying about all the things I need to do when I get to the office, is a great feeling. This is just a short list of what I gained and still gaining by meditating daily. I'm sure at this point you're curious as to how to start meditating? I'm going to make it as easy as it gets to start today. It's called guided meditation.

Guided meditation is where someone instructs you what to do from beginning to the end of your session. All you have to do is focus on doing what you're being instructed to do. The app I discovered is called Headspace and I still use it today. I believe there is a free trial and then $99.00 for the year. It will be the best $99.00 you spend. Inside the app it can be overwhelming with choices, so let me guide you to what I found that has brought me to where I am today. Inside the app, go to the bottom and hit the explore button. At the top is a box that says Meditation Basics and Timers. Open that up. Scroll down to where you see the word Basics, Basics 2, and Basics 3. Go to basics to start. Once you complete Basics, move on to basics 2 and then 3. In basics it gives you the choice to go 3 minutes to 10 minutes. Start with 3 and as you become more comfortable move up. Keep moving up until you eventually get to 20 min which is only offered in basics 3. 20 will me the max you will ever need to use in this app. Once you complete basics 3 go back to explore.

Find the box that says Stress and Anxiety. Scroll down and find the course, Managing Anxiety. It's a 30-day course that is amazing. I know you want to jump right on that one, but please do not as it will give you a possible bad experience due to it being overwhelming. Go through basics 1,2, and 3 to learn how to mediate first. Once I completed the 30-day managing anxiety course, I tried other courses in the app. None of them helped me as much as the managing anxiety course did. And like a good book, each time you read it again you get something new from it.

To this day, I continue to repeat that same course over and over again and I learn more and more as my anxiety gets under control. Each time I go through the course, I hear the instructor with a different set of ears and what he says makes my relationship with anxiety that much better. Let me share with you a few quotes from the instructor he addressed before we meditated. He always starts the sessions with a quote that has helped me look at anxiety through a different set of eyes. He stated before one session that when we train in awareness, we become more aware of everything: joy, anger, anxiety. It is all equally valuable, none better than the other. Another one is that we're not ignoring, chasing or rejecting thoughts. We're seeing them clearly, acknowledging them and letting them go. The final one that I love is, when we resist a thought, an emotion, or a circumstance, we reject life as it is. This creates further tension and suffering in the mind. My deepest hope and desire for you is to accept and put into practice meditating immediately. Other than my own experience, Google the effects of meditation on anxiety. You will see that it has been proven extensively by studies and science to reduce anxiety. I want you to take action now and download the app Headspace and start reaping the benefits sooner than I did.

CHAPTER 7

Journaling
(Good and Bad Days)

When anxiety first showed up in my life January 8th 2018, it was easily labeled a bad day. Under normal circumstances, we all mentally label a day as good or bad. You can easily find people stating how bad their day was as they list all the details that justify that label. It's very common to come home from work and your spouse or significant other asks, "How was your day?" Parents often pose the same question to their kids. These questions trigger an immediate replay of the day asking our mind to give an answer. Since the day has already happened, it's easy to come to the conclusion that it was either good or bad.

Now, if someone were to ask you about last Tuesday, for example, the answer would not come to you as easy. You would have to go back in your mind and process exactly what happened that day and if anything out of the norm happened. Most of the time, the answer would be, "Ok as far as I can remember." Good and bad days are something we don't give much thought to, **past the day itself,** until we start experiencing consecutive bad days.

It is at that moment that we start focusing on the fact that we are continuously having bad days. Eventually, this leads to thinking and labeling most days as bad even though this may not be the case. The bad days may outnumber the good days, but our mind starts to blur it all together into the belief that each day is a bad day. Over a period of time, you can become hardwired to accepting each day is going to be bad and that this is the norm. Accepting and expecting that every day is going to be a bad day, is a place **you don't want to go or live your life**.

Once you are in a place mentally that each day is going to be bad, it can sometimes be a long road back. When my anxiety began to surface, it didn't come and go, it was constant. The morning was the worst. The evening was a little less severe, but it was always dialed up. I feared going to bed knowing I was barely going to sleep. I knew I was going to lie there all night, alone with my thoughts, which increased my fear. Although they were rare, to my knowledge, there were some days I would get up and have a **better day.**

I remember telling my wife on those days, I didn't want the day to end. I feared waking up the next day and being back to feeling bad again. A few days would pass of having several bad days in a row, and it was as if the better day had never occurred, as my conscious mind could only recall having nothing, but bad days. This perception grew as the months went by and became ingrained into my thoughts. It was terrifying for me to think I was going to have to live the rest of my life like this.

I gave the perception stronghold more strength by talking about it constantly. Anyone that would listen within my trusted group, would hear how bad I felt. My family would grow weary at times of hearing me constantly talk about my bad days and when this would end. My wife offered support the best way she knew, by trying to point out the good things that were happening around me. However, anxiety leaves no space in the mind, for you to rationally process and accept this. My mother would offer support, by trying to direct my attention to accepting that this may be how I have to live the rest of my life. She would point out that many people are in worse situations than I was.

Anxiety did not allow me to rationalize the truth in this statement so I could find comfort. Unless you have ever experienced anxiety on this level, it's very difficult to understand. It's almost next to impossible to explain to someone, which makes the bad days and feeling that you are all alone, even greater. I was in desperate need of somehow feeling that everyday wasn't a bad day. I would frequently schedule visits with my doctor and good friend, Dr. Bruce Daniels.

My visits were more for comfort and trying to find an understanding than anything else. He would check me out, maybe run a new test on something we hadn't tested yet mainly to appease me. During one of my visits that I will never forget, we had a conversation about my thought that every day was going to be bad. He asked me if I thought I ever had a good or better day compared to what had become the norm of having bad days? I was able to logically say I think I have had a few, but don't remember much about them. What he told me next, I had no idea, would be another step on the road to recovery. Dr. Bruce told me to go home and on my calendar, write down every time I have a better day than the perceived bad day. He encouraged me to simply write, "Better Day" under the day it occurs.

The goal is to string a couple of better days together, to start acknowledging you do have better days. I took it a step further. As the days went on, I started to feel as if everyday was a bad day again. I would then look at my calendar to see the last time I had a better day. Once I had a few good days logged on my calendar, I started to examine how far apart the better days were from each other. Studying the good days, shifted my focus. It helped me to go back and review what made that day better.

What actions have I taken? What food had I eaten? Did I sleep better that night? I know reading this sounds like a person that is off the chart, micro analyzing his day to determine what made it better. I will say to that...it is. However, it also shifted my thoughts from all the bad I felt during a day to program my mind to recognize that there are better days. I needed to focus on what made it a better day.

I would rather be focused on that one good day and what possibly contributed to it, than all the negative that goes into the thought of having a bad day. I basically turned my focus around 180 degrees. After a few months, I started noticing the better days were happening closer and closer together, as I would look over my calendar. This gave me hope and motivation to continue my focus on the actions that made those days better. Then, something strange happened, I started having two better days in a row, then three. Then, I would have a set back of three bad days. A pattern had emerged. This made me set a more specific goal, to now have three better days in a row, and then four, until I would only have set backs occasionally.

Remember, we aren't trying to get rid of anxiety, but build a relationship with it. Once I started having more good days than bad, I stopped logging my better days and went on with life. Bad mistake. It's like not finishing all of your medicine once you start to feel better. What happens? The sickness can return quickly. I was going along with my life and bam! A really bad day came back to visit me. And then another, and another. I found myself heading down a road I knew all too well. That's when I decided this cannot be a task that I do only until I feel better. It has to be a lifelong commitment to recognize better days over bad days.

Journaling is a word I have never been fond of. I thought it was too much like a diary. That relates to spending 30 minutes to an hour writing, which is something I didn't and will not do. So, I came up with my own five-minute anxiety journaling technique that I do every night at the end of the day. It's quick and highly effective at breaking the loop of anxiety that the bad days are not getting any better. It allows you to look back and note your last good day and proving to yourself that you do have good days. It allows you to move forward, knowing if you can have one good day, you can have two good days and build on that.

Let me now explain to you where my journey took me, in regards to better days, good days, and great days. When I first started my anxiety journaling technique, I had a place at the top of the page for the date and then a blank line to rate my day. The rating system was to label the day as a bad day, better day, good day, or great day. A bad day was when I would feel like I was out of commission and could not be in a public place because my anxiety level was high. A better day is when I would waiver in and out of my anxiety all day long and had to really focus on keeping it together. A good day would be my anxiety was present, but as the day went on, by 3:00 p.m. I was what I considered, (at the time), calm and functional on a consistent basis.

On a great day, I would wake up not dialed up. Even though I was constantly looking for it to switch, the day stayed dialed down. As time went on and I would evaluate each day, the focus to pick a label for what kind of day I had, became a task in itself. There were days that could be labeled better or good and trying to decide, would raise my anxiety levels. One night, when I was praying, it came to me. God put something on my mind my mother had already pointed out to me a few months back, but it didn't stick.

Sometimes, we have to turn our focus away from ourselves and notice people all around us are suffering from many different things and recognize that some would gladly trade places with you. Suffering is a shared human experience, it's not just us. I know this is easier said than done when you're in the middle of the storm. For a long time, I could not imagine that anyone was feeling like I was. I then placed my focus on what I already knew, but never gave it much thought. There are people in the world better off than me and worse off than me. It's always been this way and it always will. What I'm asking you to do, is bring this thought to the front of your attention and really let it sink in.

Maybe you were like me and had every test there is given to you by different doctors, in order to see what's wrong and they all came back positive. <u>That means, internally you are healthy right? You wake up each day and are able to get yourself physically out of bed and walk. You are not physically handicapped, but healthy. You wake up every day breathing and get to experience another day God created.</u>

Even though you may not feel the way you would prefer to experience these things, you still get to experience them. I believe as I'm writing this book, that God laid this on my heart. I know you may not feel this way, but there is no bad day or better day. There are good days and great days.

The days you wake up not feeling yourself and your anxiety is dialed up, is still a good day because you get to experience the things I mentioned above, that others don't. On days your anxiety is dialed down and you feel more like yourself, combined with all the things I mentioned above, is a great day and you should be thankful you got to experience that. Even if you never get to experience another great day in your life, stopping and being present in the moment of that day and truly being thankful for it, starts to change things mentally.

We start to identify differently with each day. You start to label each day as good or great. And this starts to program the subconscious mind to never have bad or better days, only good or great days. Remember, the subconscious is an unquestioning servant who works day and night to make your behavior fit a pattern, consistent with your emotionalized thoughts, hopes and desires.

By listing every day in your journal you had as either a good day or a great day, makes this eventually show up in your life. I will share with you since I started this way of journaling over four months ago, at the time this book was written, it had become extremely hard for me to write down the words "good day" anymore. I have to search for a reason to label it a good day. All I can come up with after a short review of my day, is that it was a "great day." Read that again. Even if I have a slightly dialed up anxiety day, some things didn't go my way, or my day was just not up to speed, mentally, I can't write the words good day anymore, only great day.

This didn't happen overnight and I can't remember the exact day I stopped and realized that I hadn't written down the words good day in a long time. The only way I was able to remember the last time I wrote down the words good day, was to look back on my journal until I found a page that said, "good day." Let me be clear about something. I may still have had a bad day, but my mind no longer recognized it as bad because that word is no longer used to describe my day. My mind only recognizes and acknowledges the great things that happened in my day, even if it's as simple as I got to experience another day God created. That, my friend, is true change in the mind. When your mind only sees great days, anxiety starts to lose its power.

I want you to start experiencing good and great days and one day wake up and notice that you've been having nothing, but great days. I know right now that may be hard for you to believe. I promise, I do understand. I was right where you are now at one time. The good news is I'm now giving you this tool I created that took me four months to figure out, that you can start implementing today. Just do it. Get a notebook. Right now, I am asking you to put the date at the top and next to the date, at the end of the day, write good day or great day.

There will be many days at first when you write good day because in your mind, it's as close to the words bad day as you can get, if using my technique. You have to stop looking at yourself and turn your focus to the outside world and all the suffering many are experiencing. When you start doing this on a daily basis, you start to see and believe you did in fact have a good day compared to other situations. Eventually, the day will come when it is a little brighter and you have laughed for the first time in a long time. That's the day you will write great day. And that is the beginning of a life filled with many great days.

CHAPTER 8

Gratitude and Fear

I was on one of my visits with my good friend Dr. Bruce being evaluated to see if I had been getting better since the last time I saw him. During this visit, in typical Dr. Bruce wisdom, he tells a story about how more people than ever before in his career, have anxiety. He told me he was speaking with his father and his father said, *"In a world where we have so much more than ever before, we are more unhappy than ever."* I left his office, but his father's words, stayed with me. I'm going to be totally transparent here and share what my thinking was at this time, in hopes that you can relate in some way.

I was brought up very poor and me and my mom went without the things in life most take for granted. I was barely a "C" student and had dyslexia, which back then was not diagnosed. I processed things in my mind differently than the other kids, which caused me to struggle in all areas of my life. After barely graduating high school, I tried college because that's what most kids graduating high school are told they should do in order to be successful. As much as I tried, I was not college material. I went my own way under heavy criticism, into the fitness world. I loved it! And without a game plan, I wanted to somehow make a career out of it. I started off competing in bodybuilding competitions and won my very first Mr. Teenage Oklahoma. I was hooked.

I went on to win Mr. Oklahoma titles two times in the light heavyweight division and once in the heavyweight division. Once my bodybuilding career was coming to an end, I became a personal trainer and a dietary therapist. My personal training career took off and my passion for changing people's lives grew, along with my business. After a few years, I took my personal training career and turned it into a very unique, group, personal training system using only 5lb dumbbells and 40-minute workouts, that is known today as Garza's Fat Loss Camp's www.travisgarza.com. There are six locations in Oklahoma, six locations in Illinois, one location in Indiana and a LIVE broadcast workout system that reaches all over the world. www.athometransformationlive.com

I remember my first goal was to make six figures and when that day came, I would have made it in my eyes. That day arrived and I felt happy and accomplished about a goal I had longed for. Surprisingly, that feeling passed a lot quicker than I had envisioned it would. I thought, once I reached that goal, life would be good and complete.

After about a month, I began to experience fear and started having restless nights. I decided what I needed was to set a new goal. The goal was to be a millionaire by the time I was 50 years old and when I brought it to people's attention, a lot of folks laughed at me. By the age of 49, I made my first million and to add to the victory I beat my goal of doing it by the time I was 50. That day, I remember breathing out with relief saying to myself now you can be content and at ease. Unfortunately, that was not the case after a few weeks, the feeling of fear and the restless nights returned.

I often asked myself, *"Travis what are you fearing and restless about?"* I then decided I would make two million and put that in my sights for the next goal. The following year, I achieved it. Again, after a few weeks, the fear and restless nights returned. I then decided I wanted to create my own supplement line called Myosculpt Nutrition, LLC. The main drive to do this is because I was tired of the FDA not regulating supplement companies. Most companies make false label claims of what was actually in their products and getting away with it. www.garzassportsnutrition.com.

I put a lot of time and effort into creating this line and was very proud on the day we released it. The supplement line was immediately a success and people from all over were placing orders. It was now time to set a new goal. I started working on opening an actual brick and mortar store, Garza's Wholesale Sports Nutrition, in Edmond, OK. From the day it opened, it has been a success. Personally, I am married to a great woman, Adrea and have three amazing daughters Sydney, Haven and Koti, along with two dogs, Charlie and Sadi. I have an amazing mother Anne, sister Bea Jaye, niece Hannah, brother-in-law Chris and good friend and husband to my mother Max.

I live in a great neighborhood, in a great house and own two H2 Hummers, my favorite vehicle. I do not tell you all this to brag. I tell you this to make a point. Back to the words of Dr. Bruce's dad, "In a world where **we have so much** more than ever before, we are

more unhappy than ever." It took me several months, a lot of self-examination, meditation, and reading several books to finally discover something I have never done in my life. Express gratitude.

If you were to ask me pre-anxiety, if I was grateful for what I had achieved along with having an amazing family, I would have told you, "Yes, of course I'm grateful," and I give all the credit to Jesus Christ. I would have told you that the odds of a kid raised very poor, who had dyslexia, was barely a C student, and without a college education, could rise to live the life I live today, were not in his favor. That's why I give credit for my life, solely to Jesus Christ. Because without His hand guiding me, it would have never happened. That is, in one sense, being grateful. It's the sense most of us actually recognize as being grateful. The problem is that most of us miss what being grateful truly is. We are chasing a goal, dream, or thing. Most, if not all of that goal, dream, or thing, is powered by your envy of what someone else already has or achieved, that you feel you must also have in order to feel validated.

I will be the first to step forward and admit, that was me pre-anxiety. My envy was disguised. It took several months into my anxiety, when it was at its peak, to uncover. Envy can come in many forms, but the most recognized is when we envy someone's new car, house, boat, lifestyle, perfect family, or vacations. These are the most noted forms of envy. For me, my envy was based on the achievement of something and it was never about the financial outcome of that achievement. The achievement would validate a deep insecurity of "feeling less than," that stemmed from being poor a good portion of my life.

When you are truly poor and see other kids living a life you feel you will never live, you feel inadequate, less than and develop a deep insecurity about yourself. My achievements were all fear-driven. The fear of going back to being inadequate and less than other men. My subconscious was programmed to find a way for me to be the best at whatever I was striving to achieve, in order to stand out and fill that need to be validated as worthy. Worthy to walk among men that were better than me in my eyes. Men that had great jobs, took care of their families, provided a great life for their kids and were held in high respect for who they were. That was my envy. And as I accomplished more and more, my standard of what I needed to achieve, grew and grew.

As I stated earlier, it was never and still today, is not about making more money for me. I know that sounds crazy, but money didn't drive me achievement did. As I would achieve, I would attend masterminds with people doing much better than me. That was my entire reason to attend a mastermind, to surround myself with people doing better than me, so it would make me step up my game to be more successful. The only problem is that after years of being in multiple masterminds, I never consciously looked at those mentors of mine and said, "I envy them and want to be just like them."

I learned from them and applied what I learned to my own businesses. Subconsciously, I had nowhere to go, but up to what they had achieved to keep that fear of feeling less than away. After years of achieving one goal after the other, continually raising the bar on myself, add the stress and energy required to achieve that new goal, along with it all being fear driven, eventually, I woke up and found myself on my knees from extreme anxiety.

Some people would view my description as the way most every successful person succeeds. Set the bar high and work to achieve it. This is true, but there is a healthy way to do it and the way I was doing it, was not. I was being driven by fear of what would happen if I didn't achieve that next level and I was only happy when the goal was achieved. The healthy way to do it is what I learned through meditation. *"We move forward in life by knowing our goal. But we are **(happy and free as we go)**, when our happiness in NOT dependent on reaching that goal."*

Every human at some level suffers from comparison syndrome, which leads to your mind creating a goal for you to achieve, a dream to fulfill, or a thing to acquire based on your envy. After several months of pondering on Dr. Bruce's dad's statement, I came to the conclusion that comparison syndrome is why we are more unhappy than ever. It is why I was more unhappy than I had ever been and didn't even know it.

We compare and then we go out and get it. We use all means to obtain what we feel we need, based on the comparison rationalized in our mind. We may work long hours, neglect our family, take out loans, max out credit cards, or even take on a second job. We will do whatever it takes, even at the expense of adding additional stress to our life, to level the playing field to that which we are comparing. Once we acquire the goal, the dream, or the thing, we then move on to the next comparison and start the cycle all over again. Never satisfied, always stressed and never truly happy. This in return causes fear to rise in the form of, "What if I don't get or achieve a certain thing," which then leads to major anxiety.

Comparison syndrome is higher today due to social media and the ability to look inside total strangers lives and see how they live. The problem is people are posting only what they want you to see, or believe, is going on in their life. As my pastor Craig Groeschel once said, *"People are only showing you the highlight reel of their life."* They are portraying to you the house they have, the car they drive, the perfect family and the perfect vacation. What they aren't showing you, is the possible debt they are in, the car that's leased, the vacation home that is rented, or the family when it's not so perfect. In the statement above, "We move forward in life by knowing our goal. But we are *(happy and free as we go)* when our happiness in NOT dependent on reaching that goal."

The words happy and free as we go is based on true gratitude. Gratitude and fear cannot co-exist. When I learned of this, I got really excited. I've lived with fear all my life and was ready to let it go. Gratitude is the opposite of envy. Instead of wishing you had more or achieved more, shift your focus on what matters and that's to be thankful for what you already have. There is nothing wrong with wanting to do better or achieve goals, as long as your happiness is not based solely on when those goals are accomplished.

When you start practicing gratitude and it is a daily practice just like meditation, you start to realize that all the things that make you truly happy in life are so small and inexpensive. Over months of practicing daily gratitude, I found that I was grateful for things I never in my life took the time to notice, be present with and feel grateful for. My gratitude list consists of having a great wife, three healthy and amazing daughters that I love more than ever, just being around. I'm grateful for having a great mom I can talk to daily. I'm grateful for my Mother's husband Max for being a great husband to her and a good friend to me. I'm grateful I have an amazing sister, niece and brother-in- law that are in my life. I'm grateful that I can afford to eat at any restaurant I want to. I'm grateful I work doing something I absolutely love. I'm grateful for my two dogs that for the first time in my life, I'm crazy about.

I'm grateful I can get up and go workout three days per week. As time goes on, my list gets longer and longer and it feels amazing. With all that I just listed I'm grateful for, did the thought once cross your mind about my lifelong fear of being less than? The answer most likely is no. How could it? The words gratitude and love kept coming up and when those words are attached to things you truly are grateful for, fear CANNOT be present. You shut it down! And when you shut fear down, you shut anxiety down! You're to busy being grateful for what this day brings to your life and you start to forget about being afraid of not getting what "The Jones's" have on social media.

Look at the few things I listed, I'm grateful for. It made me happy typing them. You can't buy that kind of happiness. That's the true meaning of gratitude. When I first learned of practicing gratitude, it was not an easy shift of focus for me. It took time, but with determination, I changed my focus on what practicing gratitude really means and it has paid off.

I want you to experience the same happiness I now have in my life. I am still a work in progress, but I know I am on the right path and

I'm now going to get you on the same path. Practicing gratitude has two parts. The first one, I have found is best done at the end of each day. No days off. Even if you go to bed and then remember you forgot to do it, get up and do it. Each day, is one more day of programming your mind to switch from envy, which leads to stress and eventually anxiety, to that of gratitude and a calm mind. Practicing daily gratitude requires you to add to what we talked about in the last chapter, which was my five-minute anxiety journaling technique. You're doing this right? You're writing down the date on one side of the paper and the words good or great day on the other side, each day in a notebook. Next, I want you to write five different phrases with room to write under them. One of my good friends, Craig Ballantyne, gave me this concept and I use it everyday. Under the date and words good day or bad day, you will write the words I'm grateful for... then leave room to write. Don't get overwhelmed. Write down a sentence that comes to mind. Don't sit and pick your day apart trying to answer. What pops in your mind is the correct answer.

Next, write the words, "People who made a difference..." then leave room to write. Who impacted your day today? It can be one or more, the important part is to list who made a difference in your day. Next, write the words, "What I learned..." then leave room to write. What did you learn about yourself today? Did you stop and for once actually notice how calm you felt or how you responded differently to a situation? Or how beautiful that tree that's been in your front yard for five years looks? Next, write the word, "Achievements..." and then leave room to write. Pick the top five achievements of your day. It doesn't have to always be towards a goal, as people like me would tend to think. It can be something like

I meditated for 10 minutes instead of five today. I worked out today. It's whatever you consider a victory for that day. Last write the words, "#1 Priority for tomorrow..." then leave room to write.

What's number one on your list for tomorrow? You may have many, but pick the top one. For example, every Saturday night, I write going to church as my number one priority for the next day. At first, this will seem like a lot, but if you will make a template of the page and then make multiple copies, you will not have to write it all out each day. If you would like one of my pre-made compact journals that is already done for you, e-mail me at travis@travisgarza.com. The cost is $37.00 and I will ship it for FREE. This exercise should not take you more than five minutes, 10 at the most. Keep it simple, with one or two liners and use the answers that come to you immediately.

Over time, you will be able to see as you are writing these things down right before you go to bed, that they are the last things your mind processes. This in turn starts the change to being truly grateful when you look each day at what you're grateful for, who made a difference in your life, what you learned about yourself, the achievements for that day and what's your number one priority for tomorrow. The second part of being grateful is simple in context, yet hard to do for some people. The second part, which becomes highly addictive once you get into it, is adding value to someone's life each day. I admit when I first started this, I was lost. Add value to someone's life everyday? It actually becomes quite simple when you take away the, "what to buy someone" mentality, most of us perceive as adding value. I have security guards that work relentlessly at their jobs in the complex I live in.

I had been there two years and never gave those men a second thought. When I started looking around and noticing what I was grateful for, my eyes saw them. I purchased five Starbucks gift cards and I pulled my car over one day and talked to them. I told them I was thankful for what they did and it doesn't go unnoticed. I spent about 15 minutes getting to know them, even though I was behind on my schedule for the day. At that point, my schedule didn't matter. It added value and worth to their life and it was worth every minute of business I may have lost.

My wife always makes coffee in the morning and I decided since I was up earlier than her, I would get it going. That was adding value to her life, but the coffee was for us both. I then decided to make it personal and put her favorite coffee mug by the coffee machine along with her favorite protein bar. That truly added value and sent a statement to her that I took time out to notice. This became such a high for me. I made posters to put in my office over everyone's desk. It says, "Add value to someone's life today 😊." I cannot express the feeling and sense of calm you feel, by doing the simplest thing for someone else.

It doesn't always require money. A simple stop to acknowledge that person you always walk by at work, school, or even at home and telling them how much you appreciate them being in your life, goes a long way to adding value to their life. If you want to kill anxiety, this is one of the best weapons you can use. It's in our make up to focus on ourselves. We are born this way. The reason it kills anxiety is in the grand scheme of life, it's really not about you and the quicker you change your perspective on this, the quicker anxiety falls apart. When we take the focus off ourselves and focus on who we can add value to their life today, tomorrow, next week and so on, anxiety has no fuel and starts to fall apart. It's not about what can you get, but what can you give.

There is no anxiety in adding value to someone's life, only calm of mind and happiness. This chapter took me on a long painful journey that I haven't been on in awhile and I hope by being completely vulnerable and open with you, that it will truly show you what being grateful really means. My only regret is that I didn't learn the true meaning of gratitude, before I turned 52. My hope is you will not wait another day to start your own journey of finding it.

CHAPTER 9

Stressful Influences

When I was 18 and had just started my bodybuilding career, life was great. I was working in a gym, getting to workout two times a day, competing and most of all surrounded by people who were just like me. People that were heavy into the lifestyle of competing, working out and perfecting their eating habits. We all talked the same language. In a world where nobody really understood us and why we did what we did, we had each other. At the beginning of that season of my life, it was amazing. We did pretty much everything together. We hung out together outside of the gym, went on vacations together, attended each other's shows and supported each other in every situation. You could say we were one big family.

After a few years, a shift in the camaraderie began to occur. A few people started to develop negative attitudes, along with constantly speaking in a negative manner. The support for each other, changed to a competition against each other, on stage and off. The group started to split and people began to take sides based on how well one side sold their point of view to each individual. From there, the down talking began and the negativity from both sides escalated. I personally did not take sides, but was starting to feel the stress and tension. I remember especially starting to feel stressed when walking into the gym where we all were training. The one place I loved to go, was now becoming a place where negative talk, tension and stress prevailed, over motivation, stress release and good times.

These were people I truly cared about and loved as family, but something had to change. I personally still had my sights on continuing to compete and eventually starting my career fully, where I would be focusing on changing people's lives through fitness. The people I surrounded myself with for many years had become negative, stagnant and not interested in evolving to the next level of life. This was not a recipe for success in regards to what I valued most, moving forward in my life. Staying connected to people that constantly talked negative, caused stress in my life and I didn't look forward to seeing anymore, was becoming very toxic to my own way of thinking and it would eventually take a toll on my health. I had a hard decision to make. I could choose to stay in a toxic environment with loyal friends who I had shared life with, loved like family and who supported me through my own ups and downs that now stressed me out, made me unhappy and would eventually cause me to live a negative thinking lifestyle. Or, I could take the hard stance of I must leave this toxic environment and surround myself with people that I feel at peace with and support my vision of starting a career of changing people's lives through fitness.

I chose to take the hard stance and separate myself from the people I truly cared about. It wasn't easy to say goodbye to my bodybuilding family, but it had to be done. I changed gyms, places I hung out and places I would eat. A lot of criticism came with these moves, along with a lot of feelings being hurt. People who looked at me like a brother, a son and a best friend felt as if I was letting them down and it made me personally feel like I was letting them down. I could easily see how they perceived this. To them, I took the stance of I was better than them and they were not good enough to be apart of my future vision. I remember the first day I started working out at a gym and I immediately felt at peace on my drive there. I wasn't worried about any of the old gang being there and what negative talk they would speak or negative mood they would be in that day.

I wasn't thinking about how I would respond to their negative talk and questions. I felt like a weight had been lifted off my shoulders and I could once again, enjoy working out stress free. Along with all the other things I removed from my life to rid myself of this negativity, I found my mind clear, my happiness restored and my vision and drive stronger than ever. This action, as hard as it was, would be an action I would revisit later in my life to serve a different purpose. That Monday, January 8th 2018, when I found anxiety, the last thing on my mind, as one of the causes of my anxiety, was the people I was associating with and the atmosphere I had created of not saying no to myself and others. It took me several months to figure out these things were a major contributor to my anxiety. It was a slow build up over time, that I wasn't paying attention to and eventually it boiled over.

When my anxiety was at its highest in the beginning, I became very sensitive to the things that would make it worse or better. Driving to a headquarters meeting would cause my anxiety to increase. On my drive home from work, my anxiety would lessen. Being in certain environments, would also dictate the increase or decrease, of my anxiety. Being in airports would increase my anxiety. Being outside doing work around the house, would make my anxiety go down. The one thing I noticed that really increased my anxiety the most, was the days leading up to a certain event I attended every three months. I found that my anxiety would be at its worst and it was an event I loved, so at first I was looking everywhere I could, for the reason for the increase in my anxiety, except the event itself. The event was created for only 10-15 high performing people in my field of work and was used to inspire you by gaining new ideas from others in that field. The objective was to send you back home with a positive mindset and action plan.

It was a brotherhood of like-minded people, that I had spent years with putting our minds together to better ourselves. I then decided to ask myself this simple question, *"Travis what about this environment **you're going to put yourself in,** do you not like?"* Immediately, I had given my mind the ok, to focus on the actual event for once and provide the answer. My anxiety didn't go up because of the event itself, my anxiety went up because of certain people at the event, I dreaded interacting with. People in retrospect, I didn't want to associate with and had blocked out mentally. Not because they were bad people, but they were always griping and complaining about what wasn't working and constant negative talk about their life. I found myself not preparing for the event with a positive attitude, but focusing on who I was hoping would not be in attendance. This should have been my first red flag months before my anxiety struck.

Instead of focusing on what I could bring to the table at the event, I was dreading who would be there to suck all the energy out of me. Does this story sound familiar to you? It's the same story I experienced in my early twenties when I would be driving to the gym and dreading it. Now I was experiencing it again in my fifties. I remember telling my wife, I couldn't go to the scheduled event because I was feeling so bad from my anxiety being dialed up. She knew I had to really be feeling bad to miss this event because I loved going to it. We both decided I shouldn't go and I made the call. Within hours of making that call, I felt so much better and a sense of relief. That's when I started my self-examination of why I felt better. It took me a week of self-talk about the event and what made my anxiety go up, to find the answer. Once I got past how much I loved going to the event itself, the answer came to me clearly.

I had attended this group for many years with so many great things coming from it. The three to five negative people in it, who came to complain every three months about everything, had taken its toll on me. The negative talk was all that I was leaving the event with. I was no longer feeling inspired or positive about being apart of this group and it was time to leave. I felt like the story a fisher man once told. He said if you take a bucket and fill it with crabs, you don't have to worry about putting a lid on it. Your first thought is the crabs will crawl out if you leave the lid off. The fact is, the crabs will all walk around slowly in a sort of circle formation. Sooner or later, one crab will try to step on top of the other crabs, to get out. As soon as the ambitious crab does this, all the other crabs will get excited and come close together, reaching up with their claws and pulling him back down with the rest of them. They will then resume slowly going in the circle. It was hard to leave this group. I have made many friendships through it just as I did with my bodybuilding family, but it had to be done.

I left the group on good terms, wishing everyone in that group nothing but success. As a side note, this one event I attended was not the sole cause of my anxiety to surface. It was a combination of things, but this was one I could let go of without repercussion and would put me one step in the right direction of healing. I'm not one to avoid personal or professional growth just because it is stressful. This would be a step back and regroup from my goal of connecting with like-minded, positive people. Positive stress **doesn't** typically cause friction in the mind, which leads to anxiety. It's the stress of trying to avoid the negativity of certain people who tend to be time vampires over a period of time, that causes the friction in the mind. Time vampires can come in two forms. The first form are people who suck you dry of energy constantly needing something from you or wanting you to listen to their complaints.

You know immediately when you see them, that they already have something to ask of you or are dying to tell you how bad their day was...again. The second form, is self-inflicted. Not being able to say no. It's a hard word for most to say, especially to someone when asked to do something and in my case saying no, in regards to taking on too many projects. I had to put boundaries in my work and personal life. I had to learn to say no to the things that didn't align with what I valued and let go of what I really didn't value. In my work life, I had to quit taking on so many projects at one time. When we have multiple projects going on, we don't do a really good job on any of them. I considered myself a master at multitasking. When we multitask, we are torn in multiple directions, which causes (underlying) anxiety and constant worry (a contributor to anxiety), of trying to complete them all.

The time vampire of multiple projects come in and suck you dry of your energy and mental health. When we limit ourselves to one, maybe two projects, two things increase. We can be more focused and more creative because we have our sights on one maybe two, at the most, topics. Pick the project that most needs your attention and give your full focus on completing it. I found by doing one project at a time with my full focus, that I actually get more projects completed at a higher quality than I did when I would take on three to five projects at once.

My stress went down along with my anxiety and the feeling of accomplishment I experience is much higher, since I took this approach. As a bonus, I'm more motivated than ever for the next project. I had to learn that most projects can be listed in order from most to least important and when you can approach your projects like this, it's a much more enjoyable ride. The next project can wait and the world will not come to an end. In my personal life, I had to pick what I valued to focus my energy on and let go of those things I didn't. I had to realize that I didn't have to be involved with everything going on in my household. Pre-anxiety, I felt responsible for making sure I was involved with everything going on and being completed at home. For a recent example, I will use my wife's remodeling of the kitchen. Pre-anxiety, I would have wanted to be in on what colors the wall was going to be, the tile being put down on the floor and what we were going to do for a kitchen while the kitchen was being remodeled. Not to be controlling, but feeling I needed to participate. Post anxiety, I stopped myself and asked the question, "How much do you really value the way this kitchen turns out?"

The answer was I don't. This doesn't mean I don't care, it simply means my wife values the remodel of the kitchen 10 times more than I do and I trust her with overseeing this project. It was energy and unnecessary stress I didn't have to add to my daily life. I had a choice to add this stress to my life, which leads to anxiety or step away and enjoy the process of just watching the new kitchen come alive. There are things in my household that I feel are my responsibility, which are not an option for me. For example, making all three of my girls Sydney, Koti and Haven breakfast, packing their lunch for school and giving my three-year-old twins a bath each night. I value what my girls eat. Being involved with the remodel of the kitchen, I did not.

I had the option with the kitchen and that is the key point I'm making. There are responsibilities that we **don't have** an option to do, that cause us anxiety. Then there are those things that **we do have an option** to do that cause us anxiety. Find the things that cause your anxiety to go up and you have an option to do and step away from them. By finding these things and stepping away from them, you automatically reduce your anxiety, which will help reduce your anxiety with the things you can't step away from that are your responsibility. You have to learn to say no to yourself as I explained and say no to others. That person that seeks you out to ask something of you and causes you anxiety you have to learn to say no to them.

If you get asked to go out on the town and that thought causes you anxiety, you have to learn to simply say, "No thank you." That person that wants to complain to you about how bad their day is everyday and causes you anxiety, you have to learn to say no. Will you hurt some people's feelings? Probably, but your health is the priority right now and if saying no causes you to lose a friend, they weren't really friends to begin with. I had to learn this the hard way because I kept allowing these people into my world. Now if someone approaches me and I can sense that it is going to be negative, I tell them I have five minutes and I have somewhere to be. I stand by that five minutes and then when the five minutes are up, I tell them, I hope they have a great day, but I have to go. Set hard boundaries so you can take those necessary steps to healing.

I don't want you to take several months to figure this out like I did. The action I'm going to ask you to take will probably be one of the hardest things for you to do, but is completely necessary if you want to get healthy. It was definitely one of the hardest things I had to do, but has contributed on a large scale to getting my anxiety under control. It's hard because it involves people you know and may be close to and possibly leave you feeling or being made to feel like you are letting them down. I want you to do this exercise that helped me tremendously create a more peaceful and better quality of life. Schedule a time for yourself, when you will be alone and can truly self-exam your life. You will need a pen and pad to write on. You need to first reflect on the people and environments that cause the most stress and anxiety in your life and also identify what gives you relief. Once you have identified these, you need to write them down. It's not enough to just think about them. You need to make a list of people and environments that cause you the most stress and what gives you relief.

The path forward becomes simple. Avoid the things that make you anxious and focus more on the things that calm you down. Every day, you must learn to eliminate the triggers that cause anxiety to arise and add more (routines and habits) that support your success and reduce stress. To accomplish this, you must put certain boundaries in place. Non-negotiable boundaries. You have to make hard decisions about what you are willing and not willing to do. You must look at the fact that every environment you're in is your personal responsibility. If you want to rid yourself of anxiety, you can't continue doing what you have always done that causes anxiety.

I understand there are many things and responsibilities we have to do that are out of our control that can cause us anxiety. It's about removing the things that are in our control that cause anxiety. We do have a choice and can remove it. You may have to leave that group of loved ones like I had to, that do not serve your best interest anymore. You may have to find a different job, if the one you have now contributes on a large scale to your anxiety. You may have to leave that relationship that is not healthy and causing you daily anxiety being in it. There is no easy way out with some of these decisions and taking action can be painful for all involved. But this is one time I pray you will put yourself and your health first. Now let's go make that list and take action immediately towards changes that will lead to less anxiety in your life.

CHAPTER 10

When Is It Going To End?

I believe everything in life that we interpret as bad, our thought process brings the question when is it going to end? When everything is going good, that question never crosses our mind. When we are having an amazing day with our family on a Saturday, we never stop and ask, when is this amazing day going to end? We are simply present in the moment and only thoughts of thankfulness come to our mind. It's completely normal when you are living in discomfort, to want it to go away and start to question when it will end. Our mind is simply trying to find a solution to make this discomfort go away. The mind's job is and always will be, to keep the body in homeostasis or the ability to maintain a state of internal balance and physical well-being.

Sadly, in many situations, this question does not get answered as fast. If the discomfort continues for a long period of time, it is very easy to become fixated on that question of when it is going to end. This causes you to start to lose touch with everything else going on around you. You become fixated day after day with this question. Over time, you will start playing scenarios over and over in your mind with regards to how you may have to live your life with this discomfort. Although these scenarios haven't happened yet, they will cause fear to arise in the mind as if they actually are. The fact that you are asking the question of when is it going to end, provides you with scenarios prematurely. You begin to think about how you will live with the discomfort before it even begins. This is when fear can take root in your mind. Once embedded, it can be a very difficult task to find your way to reality, if left unaddressed. One surefire way to remain stable is to be present.

In this regard, here is how I break down fear, F.E.A.R. is False Evidence Appearing Real. Fear is an emotion we all have and we all need. However, in this case, it's being called upon based on F.E.A.R. The mind is bringing up scenarios that have not happened yet. While this may be the case, it also simultaneously activates the emotion of fear to address the scenario. You have to consciously focus on what's really happening at this moment in your life and let tomorrow take care of itself. Once we can recognize False Evidence Appearing Real, which is typically future-related because it is based on something that hasn't happened yet; we can bring ourselves back to the actual moment of what's going on in our life right now and our fear decreases to a low level that is easily managed. False Evidence Appearing Real in regards to the future, is a shared human experience that most deal with daily.

Until I found anxiety, I lived my whole life based on F.E.A.R. Every scenario of an outcome in any situation, personal or business, I created. I would play each scenario over and over again and as time grew closer to knowing the outcome, the scenario would change slightly or new ones would arise. I was causing fear in my life trying to do what only God can do and that is to know what my future was. I had to train myself to think differently, if I was going to remove the fear in my life, which leads to anxiety. The new approach to my task or situations in my personal life and business, is to make the best informed decisions along with taking the best calculated steps possible towards a great outcome.

The key to being content and losing the fear, is to know I have done my very best to create a favorable outcome. There is a sense of calm when you can actually believe this about yourself regardless of the outcome. Up until now, I have used the words, "living in discomfort," with regards to the question of when is it going to end? I did this purposely to set the background, so you better understand my personal experience of living with this question. I hope to expand your mind so that it recognizes this can be applied to any situation involving living in discomfort being with yourself, or someone you know with a different meaning to living in discomfort than yourself. Living in discomfort of any sort can cause anxiety. Having anxiety to begin with, which eventually causes discomfort in the body, only adds anxiety on top of anxiety. That day on January 8th, 2018, when I woke up knowing something was wrong, my entire focus was strictly directed to figuring out what was happening to me.

The emotion of fear had definitely presented itself, but I was at full strength mentally and physically at this time. I had thoughts such as this will pass, you need some rest, it's been a stressful week and no need to panic. I was still able to fight mentally and as I've mentioned earlier, found no need to bring this to anyone else's attention. As the weeks went by and the unknown of what was happening to me wasn't getting any better, my concern of what was going on, started to become my focus. After a few months, I decided to go to Dr. Bruce to explain my situation looking for the answer to (end) this unknown feeling. I opened up to my wife, mom, and sister making them vow total silence about my situation as we worked together to find a solution to (end) this. I even made them vow to keep this from Sydney, my 14-year-old daughter to protect her from worrying about me.

As the months went by, I eventually started to weaken mentally and physically. The constant battle of looking for answers to (end) the unknown was marked by repeat visits to Dr. Bruce for a different test. I was constantly reading Google about everything that had my symptoms along with looking for the cure for it all the time. Between reading Google obsessively to having moments of it will get better, it started to take its toll on my life mentally and physically. I had become a shell of the man I used to be and I was completely aware of it. My strength was gone physically and I had lost my will to workout along with my will to fight for a solution was all, but gone. Fear had taken control of my mind and the scenario surfaced that this is the way the rest of your life will be until this (ends). I had no game plan, no answers and no more ideas. This all left me with a few things to think about and ask the question, when will this end God? What is wrong with me? What did I do to deserve this? This is when I used the phrase, "You're at rock bottom," to describe myself. I played out my life and how it would be living like this. I was accepting defeat. There was no use in carrying on or doing anything else until this ends.

I was miserable, didn't feel good and had no energy. My whole existence revolved around the thought that I could live my life again once the unknown I was experiencing, ended. I had caused time to stand still in my life, my wife's life, my mom's life and to some extent, all those I impacted in everyday life by having this one thought on my mind every waking moment. When is it going to end?! Looking back, I view it as sitting down and putting my life on hold emotionally with myself, my family and business until the unknown went away. I locked myself into a mental solitary confinement.

That day at the Heart Hospital, after thousands of dollars of tests revealing nothing was wrong with me and that I had anxiety, it would represent the beginning of letting go of the question when is it going to end. I now knew what I had after reading everything that pointed to anxiety. I was the poster child for it on a high level. This didn't change my thoughts overnight. I had been in this thought mode for many months now and it was going to take a lot of work to dig my way out. Finally knowing what it was, relieved the fear of the unknown, which is a battle of its own. What I'm going to share with you, I hope you will take immediate action on and not spend months like I did, putting my life on hold waiting for the anxiety to end. Instead of focusing on when the anxiety will end, accept the fact that it will not. Anxiety is not a disease, it's an emotion you were born with. It's a shared human experience, much bigger than ourselves. My and your anxiety, is just dialed up a little to high. Focusing on defeating it and getting rid of it, will just cause the anxiety to dial up higher.

We want to focus on dialing down our anxiety to a level everyone else experiences in everyday life. Doesn't that sound much easier to do than getting rid of it? If we focus on getting rid of it, then we are constantly looking around, so to speak, to see if its back. If we are constantly looking around to make sure it's not back, this causes stress, fear and eventually dialed up anxiety. If it's viewed as an emotion we are all born with and as a part of our makeup, this allows room for acceptance in the mind.

It's as much of a part of your make up as your legs are. If you can look at it from this point of view, it will make more sense to the mind and allow you to start moving forward. You don't look occasionally to see if your legs are gone because it's apart of who you are. Over the years, you have built a relationship with your legs and have full control of what they do. I want you to start building a relationship with anxiety, just like you have done with your legs. Once you build that relationship, you will start having control over it just like you do with your legs. Simply put, society tries to rid you of anxiety as the answer when they should be teaching you to build a relationship with it. Be curious about it, not afraid of it.

Learn what makes it dial up and what makes it dial down. These answers are not in my book, nor will you find them in any book. That's not to say don't read what causes others anxiety to dial up that you can relate to, but ultimately search yourself and take notes of what causes your anxiety to dial up and then take the necessary corrective action. The relationship you build with anxiety is unique in nature due to the circumstances in your life being unique. It's not hard once you change your perspective as I've asked you to. Start focusing on what causes the emotion of anxiety to dial up and dial down and not when it will end. Living your life based on when something will end, is living on a future outcome, that unless you're God, you do not have the absolute answer to.

We can't live our lives hanging onto a timeframe of when the anxiety ends. We must live each day in the present and let tomorrow take care of itself. Living life in the moment, takes away the thought of when it will end. Building a relationship with anxiety causes it to fall apart. Approximately one year ago, I turned my focus to building a relationship with anxiety. I also decided, if I was going to build a relationship with anxiety and co-exist with it, I had to quit being afraid of it, but I also had to acknowledge it briefly when it's present to give my mind what it needed to move on. Trying to ignore anxiety when it starts to dial up, just makes you think about it more. The more you think about it, the more fuel you put on the fire. Think about this, imagine a strange person is staring at you in a store and you try to act like you don't notice they are staring. What happens? Your thoughts become fixated on why the person is staring at you as you try to act like you don't know they are staring. This causes major friction in the mind. However, if you stop and stare back briefly, nine times out of 10, the person will turn away and that will be the end of him or her staring at you and your mind moves on from thinking about it.

Stopping and acknowledging anxiety by saying to yourself, "Oh that's anxiety," followed by a brief pause to determine the action or thought that possibly took place to cause the anxiety to dial up, will cause anxiety to fall apart. I acknowledge it and go on with what I was doing. I no longer live with the fear of, it's back or what do I need to do to make it go away anymore. I recognize it's not going away because it is apart of who I am. I don't panic to hurry up and try and make it go away. I simply now look at anxiety with curiosity, not fear. The one thing I want you to really focus on that you will learn from meditation, is to be present in the moment. That means focus on the task at hand or being fully present and truly listening when someone is speaking to you. This was a very hard task for me to learn, but through meditation, which teaches you to focus on the breath, I am now able to do this in my daily life. By focusing on the breath only during meditation this helped me to specifically focus on the task I'm performing at the moment in my daily life.

I now look around at people and think to myself, look at what we do to ourselves. Constantly living in the past in thought and in the future in thought. Both cause a lot of stress in the mind. It doesn't surprise me that anxiety is on the rise because everyone is forgetting to live in the present. We need to learn to live in today, not yesterday or tomorrow. I'm not saying visiting yesterday or the future in your mind is bad, but do it briefly. Then come back to what's happening at this moment in your life.

Too many people spend all their time in the past or in the future, while just going through their daily life on autopilot. You were not designed to live like this. You're truly missing out on so much by not being present in the moment of this day. By spending too much time in the past or too much time in the future in thought, our mind is trying to cope with the future, past and present at the same time. This causes friction, which overtime will lead to anxiety.

When you really learn to be present in the moment, (really focused on what you are doing right now) you don't have time to think about anxiety. Once you really start to focus on being present in the moment, the day will come when you stop and realize I forgot about my anxiety. When that day happens, you know you're on the right path to a better life.

The final thing I give you that truly changed my relationship with anxiety, is along with being truly being present in the moment, was being grateful. I've already covered this, but I want to revisit it briefly. Before I get out of bed each day and before I go to bed each night, I thank God one at a time, individually, for what I am grateful for. I also write it down in my journal. By starting my day off this way and ending it this way, it keeps anxiety from even having a chance to dial up. As I stated earlier, fear and gratitude cannot exist at the same time. Start your day being grateful, being present in the moment during the day and end the day being grateful. When you're busy being present in the moment and being grateful, you don't have time for anxiety.

Chapter 11

The Band-Aid Approach

I clearly remember when I started feeling better and my anxiety had gone down. It was the beginning of February 2019 and I was on my way home from work. As I got closer to home, the normal start of my anxiety dialing up didn't occur. It was still there, but not dialed up to the level it had been for months. I even found myself slightly excited to get home and see my twin daughters. This was something that had contributed to my anxiety dialing up for over eight months. That evening at home was one of the best, I had felt in months. I couldn't remember the last time I had an evening at my house with my anxiety dialed down. As bedtime approached, the excitement of the past four hours started coming to an end. I can remember thinking I don't want to go to bed and let this feeling end. To be honest, I went to bed that night not having the highest confidence that things had changed.

The anxiety had been a dominant force in my life for over eight months and the thought of would it be there tomorrow when I woke up, was on my mind. The next morning, I opened my eyes and started to examine myself mentally. I sat up and felt noticeably better than I had over the past several months. I wasn't as dialed up, afraid, or physically feeling weak as my mornings typically were, before starting my day. I was able to control my thoughts better and not all over the place. To be clear, my anxiety didn't magically go away, but compared to the suffering I had experienced for months, it was much better. If you have ever suffered from anything for a long period of time, you know that if the suffering goes down 5%, it's like taking a breath of fresh air. My mood for the day had slightly elevated and I felt a glimpse of what it meant to be human again.

I remember driving to work and praying to God that even if this is the only day I get to feel this way, I was grateful. I wasn't going to question, or fear that tomorrow, I would be right back to feeling horrible again. I was going to focus on today and love every moment of it. I had taken for granted so many things. I was blessed to experience each hour of the day in my life even the simple enjoyment of driving to work. At work that day, I found myself enjoying being around my staff and talking to them. I still had to limit myself to how long a conversation was as this would start dialing up my anxiety. The fact that I could actually spend time, even if it was a short amount of time, talking to my staff was a great feeling. It was one more thing I had taken for granted all my life. On my drive home, there was a certain point in my drive, where when I drove by the security guards of my development, that my anxiety would start to dial up each day. This had happened like clockwork for months. This sent a message to my mind to increase my anxiety, that I was close to home and my two-year-old twins were waiting on me to act like two-year-olds.

That day, I drove by the security guards, my anxiety stayed dialed down and for the second day, the slight emotion of excitement to see my twins, arose. That evening, my anxiety stayed dialed down and I once again, enjoyed my evening with my family. The days of feeling better started to add up and my confidence started to grow. I realized I had turned a corner. Weeks went by as my anxiety dialed down even more and my confidence grew even stronger. As my confidence grew, I started to engage in life more as my anxiety was not holding me back.

I started working out to get back to the level I once was at and I took on more projects at work. I started multi-tasking in all areas of my life and found myself thinking my old life will be mine again soon. Life was heading in a good direction and I was starting to feel like I was making a comeback. I would once again be back to the old Travis functioning at the highest level and would once again be known as a machine that goes and goes and goes. I started setting new goals that I once had pre-anxiety and my focus was starting to be clear again. Then one afternoon, I noticed I started feeling a little nervous. I searched my mind on what I was nervous about, but came up empty. That night, my sleep was restless and the next morning I was exhausted. I went through my regular routine, but didn't feel so great. I chalked it up to my twins just getting over a cold and I had caught it. That day, my focus was foggy, my energy low and I felt weak.

As the days went by, I found myself starting to get anxious and the slight feeling of fear surfacing. Once these two emotions surfaced, I knew what was next. My anxiety was giving me a warning it was starting to dial up. My first thoughts were, "Why was this happening to me again?" I became angry about it returning. Then I became sad at the thought of returning to that life I thought I had left behind. After a few days of going through all these emotions and starting to feel the effects of my anxiety dialing up again, one evening I decided to pause. I told myself, Travis stop. Get control of your emotions and think this through. Face your fear and search for what has changed to cause the anxiety, to start it's path to dialing up again. Remember F.E.A.R. is False Evidence Appearing Real. Think. What changed and then address it. I started to write down what I had done and who I had spoken to over the past week, searching for what or who triggered the anxiety. I continued to come up empty over and over again.

Then in a moment of exhaustion from searching my mind, I decided to take a break and look for something to calm me down. I decided I would go meditate for 15 minutes and give my mind a break. After I meditated for 15 minutes, I immediately felt more calm, which gave me the thought I should start meditating in the evening again. At that moment when the thought to start meditating "again" in the evening crossed my mind, all the answers to why my anxiety was starting to dial up again became crystal clear. My search for why my anxiety was starting to dial up again, was in the wrong place. I was looking for someone or something that was causing my anxiety to dial up, instead of looking at myself and what I wasn't doing. When you go to the Doctor and they prescribe antibiotics, what is the first thing they say near the end of your visit and it's written on the bottle? Take all of this medication, until the bottle is empty, even if you start to feel better. By not taking all of this medication, you run the risk of the disease and sickness returning. The first reaction we as humans do, when we start to feel better is to abandon the very thing that was making us feel better. None of us don't like to think we need to be dependent on something to feel better.

We want to stand on our own two feet so to speak. For several months leading up to that day, I started feeling better. I had consistently placed in my life, all the coping strategies I have listed in each chapter of this book. I changed my entire life around in order to make sure each strategy was used on a daily basis. It was a top priority each day to make sure I didn't miss practicing each one. At first, it was a learning curve implementing each one into my already structured life. As time went on, it became the norm like anything else in life and just flowed. Somewhere I lost my way and my top priorities changed. I went from meditating 20 minutes in the morning and 15 minutes at night, to 20 minutes in the morning was good enough. I got so caught up in my evenings, that I sometimes forgot to journal good or great day, along with what I'm grateful for. Then the "sometimes not journaling" led to a lot of the times to it not being a big deal mentality. I lost focus on consistently adding value to someone's life and settled with doing it two times per week. I had started to add an extra 30 minutes past my structured bedtime I had stuck to for months.

I shifted from eating for a calm mind to eating for a calm mind with some junk food added, more often than I should. I started attending a few events with the people I knew were stressful influences from my past, but I felt like now I could separate myself from them mentally at the event. The final nail in the coffin, so to speak, is I lost sight of my values aligning with my actions. I was so blind once I started feeling better by the desire and thought to have the old Travis back pre-anxiety, that I had known all my adult life. I wanted that person that had created three successful businesses because only that person knew the path to success.

When we're sick with a cold or flu, we just wish we could feel like ourselves again and I was no different. It wasn't just stopping one of the strategies that started to dial my anxiety back up because I didn't stop any of them. It was the combination of doing each of them to a lesser degree here and there, which overall adds up to a recipe for failure over time. It's no different than my clients trying to lose weight. At first, they followed my plan to the letter and workout consistently. They get amazing results and feel the best they have in several years. Once they get these amazing results over a period of time, they start to slowly change the plan.

It starts out slowly, a little here and a little there, leaning back towards the habits that caused them to gain weight to begin with. Slowly, they start to put the weight back on, but slow enough it goes unnoticed at first. Then, the day comes when they wake up and see that they are practically back to where they first started. They had convinced themselves that they were still doing the same program, that they had success with some small changes that wouldn't be a big deal. I convinced myself that the small things I changed, to the strategies I've listed in this book would be ok and would keep producing the same result, as doing them at 100% to the best of my ability each day.

What I didn't recognize through my months of trial and error of finding strategies to dial my anxiety down, was the amazing new way of life I had created. I had stopped living in fear of the past and future and started enjoying the present day and what it had to offer. I quit worrying and started living. I slowed down and gained patience. I had found a calm I have never experienced through meditation. I found that I can still be successful by focusing on one project at a time and didn't need five to feel accomplished. I found that I don't need to burn the candle at both ends and going home early to be involved with my family was much more rewarding. I learned the work will always be there tomorrow.

I started recognizing other people by truly listening to what they were saying and not just tuning out, until they were done. I started looking at how I can add value to other people's lives, instead of rushing by and not noticing them at all. Simply put, I had found the peace and happiness of a new found way of life. Once this all became clear, I started my journey back to that new life I had found by implementing all of my strategies, back into my life on a daily basis at 100%. What I realized is my old way of life I thought I wanted back so much, is what caused me to find anxiety in the first place. Why would I want to go back to my old self I wondered? I had to change things in my life to get a different outcome. I had to accept that those changes needed to be permanent and I could not go back to that old lifestyle if getting better was my goal.

I knew that anxiety wasn't something you get rid of from my months of reading and studying. It was an emotion we all share along with others. The strategies in this book are what helped me to build a relationship with anxiety. In order to live with it, I would need to make those strategies as much a part of my life, as eating food. Since putting these strategies back in place, I am back to feeling myself again and improving each day. My perspective on my life has changed in a big way in regards to where I'm heading. I no longer want to go back to the old Travis I had longed for during that eight-month journey.

I want the Travis with the same drive, motivation and focus that built three successful businesses, but with a balance in life. The balance of having peace of mind and happiness in my life at the same time of continuing to evolve and being productive in my business. Being fully present in today and enjoying the day itself and not lost in the past or the future. Not taking one day for granted because I am not guaranteed tomorrow. To stop and have empathy for others that are suffering from anxiety and letting them know I understand what they are going through and they are not alone. It basically is living a life of it's not about me or what I think I should have or where I should be in my business to feel successful. It's about being content regardless of the emotion you are experiencing at any given moment. You can be happy or sad and still be content. It just takes practice to learn this. Also understanding that most behaviors are a human shared experience, which should cause you to have empathy towards others.

So, regardless of what you are experiencing, others experience also. And since you understand how you feel when experiencing certain things, this should bring about empathy towards others and understanding. It's much more rewarding when your focus is on adding value and relating to other people's lives, rather than being focused on yourself. The title of this chapter is, "The Band- Aid

Approach." That title came from my visit in the heart hospital when Dr. Duroy, the counselor, met with me. He spoke some words to me a few hours before I was released to go home that stuck with me.

He told me no matter what I did or medication I took, you can't control anxiety with a quick fix band-aid approach. He said you are a fast-paced person that gets things done and that has brought you a lot of success. Learning to control anxiety will be one thing you cannot take a fast-paced, get it fixed approach with. You must address the underlying issues and make changes in all areas of your life or this will not get better, it will get worse. He said society thinks taking anxiety medication will fix the anxiety.

Anxiety medication helps to mask the underlying issues, but it will not change the reason you have anxiety itself. It's a band-aid approach and until you address and make changes to the underlying issues in your life that caused you to meet anxiety, it will remain. I left the heart hospital that day, not knowing how true those words would be to me.

I feel as if God placed it on my heart to write this book because it was never in my plans to do so. Before writing this book, I had to make a decision if I wanted to expose my personal struggle with anxiety to the world and all that comes with being vulnerable. I'm a very private person and very rarely speak about my personal life. The push internally to write the book and speak publicly at events to people on this topic was too strong for it not to be from God. At first I was uncomfortable knowing that someone was going to read about the personal secret I had kept from everyone outside of my family. Then a calm came over me and I quit thinking about myself.

I started thinking about how many people I can help with what I learned through trial and error to create a relationship with anxiety. By my own words, the anxiety is an emotion that is a shared human experience. So although my journey seems unique to me, it's not. Thousands of people are going through what I went through and still are going through it. The names have changed, but the experience is the same. My hope and prayer for you is that you will use each of these tools I use on a daily basis to start your own journey to building a relationship with anxiety. Don't fear it. Don't ignore it. Don't run from it. Embrace it. Be curious about it.

Understand your goal is not to get rid of it, but to become friends with it by building a relationship with it. Like any relationship you have with someone, there are days you feel irritated by that person and then there are days you flow with them. Anxiety is no different. I want you to know that you can get your life back and like me, it can be better than before. Is it perfect? No...but what in life is? Last, I want you to know you are not alone with this. Thousands of people like you and me are going through life living with anxiety. Most are silent about the fear of being vulnerable like I was. You don't have to be silent anymore because chances are, the person next to you is being silent about it also. Open up to someone you trust and find comfort knowing you don't have to travel this journey alone.

ABOUT THE AUTHOR

It's been said that wherever he goes, Travis Garza leaves a trail of lean, fit bodies in his wake. Those who have accepted his Six Week 20lb Weight Loss Challenge will attest to the fact that this personal trainer, fat-loss expert, and founder of Garza's Fat Loss Camps is a force to be reckoned with. www.travisgarza.com

Garza entered the fitness industry in 1985 as a competitive bodybuilder, and subsequently earned the title of "Mr. Oklahoma" four times. Throughout his years as a bodybuilder, he learned first-hand how the human body responds to proper nutrition and exercise, resulting in the loss of fat for a sleek, sculpted appearance.

Armed with knowledge and fueled by a passion to help others succeed in the area of personal training, Garza used his skills as a dietary therapist to create personal eating plans based on an individual's needs. Garza went on to open his first fat loss camp in 1994 in Midwest City, Oklahoma, enabling him to reach more people in a large group setting than he could in his personal training career. This is where his signature program, The Six Week 20lb Weight Loss Challenge, www.melt20in42.com, thrust him into the public spotlight as thousands of online video success stories featuring camp attendees drew dozens of new clients on a weekly basis.

Garza's enthusiasm for fitness and his ability to communicate enthusiastically and effectively soon caught the attention of the broadcast media, where he now appears regularly on television and radio talk programs, spreading his gospel of the fitness truth to thousands. His fat-loss articles and tips have been published regularly in newspapers, magazines, and fitness equipment publications, bringing positive change to readers on a national basis.

Often referred to as "The Master of Body Transformation," Travis Garza maintains one of the highest success rates in the fitness industry. Garza's Fat Loss Camps have grown to 15 campuses total in Oklahoma and one online camp broadcast to people all over the world, with licensees in IL, ID, ATL, FL, and NC and additional locations to open in the future.

The success of The Six Week 20lb Weight Loss Challenge has given birth to additional proprietary personal weight-training programs: Elite and Hardbody. In 2014, Garza launched his own supplement line, Myosculpt Nutrition www.garzassportsnutriton.com. In January 2016, Garza opened his own brick and mortar store, Garza's Wholesale Sports Nutrition.

Travis Garza's experience and knowledge of the fitness industry are surpassed only by his ability to encourage and coach clients through his high-energy informational video sessions, available on either a weekly or daily basis, depending on the weight-training program. Garza devotees say his capacity for presenting complex nutritional, physiological, and training equipment-related information in a way that is easy to understand and adaptable is what keeps them motivated and on track.

Garza is constantly a step ahead of the industry norm by working and creating new programs that the fitness industry labels "outside of the box." Travis's online (at home) program has grown to international status, reaching people from Japan, Australia, Costa Rica, and all over the US with his patented workout formula that participants can do in the comfort of their own homes. Garza is most satisfied when he is creating or launching his new programs, which he knows will help all people achieve a better quality of life.

Travis Garza lives in Edmond, Oklahoma with his wife Adrea and three daughters, Sydney and twins Haven and Koti. He is a devoted family man who loves spending time with his wife, watching his daughter play soccer and spoiling the twins.

CONTACT THE AUTHOR

● ● ● ● ●

For Booking & To Connect With Travis

Website:
www.travisgarza.com

Email:
travis@travisgarza.com

Instagram:
@TravisGarzaOfficial

Facebook:
Travis Garza Official
https://www.facebook.com/travisgarzaofficial/

Twitter:
https://twitter.com/TravisGarza